Here's What People Are Saying about this Book

"In the land of the *glass half full/glass half empty*, we often forget that *frustration is energy* . . . Larry helps harness that energy as a positive fuel to drive your company."

George Glover, President
Wilson Hotel Management Company, Inc.

"Seeing is believing! We've used this process for the past three years. During this period we have measured dramatic improvements in teamwork and communications. I am a firm believer that frustration is a company's best friend."

Keith Riggs, Vice President
J. A. Riggs Tractor Company

"*Frustration Is Your Organization's Best Friend* is a detailed portrait of corporate America with a twist. The book includes insightful and strategic maneuvers to create a climate for success. Larry has woven through the infrastructure of firms and organizations like few have done to ensure the corporate culture is a friend to the quality improvement efforts rather than an enemy."

Terry Nichols, Operations Manager
Allen Family Foods

"This book is very readable. Cuts directly to the issues with excellent examples. It breaks 'culture' down to a bite-size common sense approach to improve your organization. Excellent! Highly recommended if you are serious about changing."

Jim O'Hanlon, Senior Vice President
Nuclear Virginia Power

"If you're tired of reading about theoretical approaches to change then you must read this book. Larry explains a unique, practical and common sense process to give every manager the opportunity to lead, manage and quantify corporate culture change."

Pat Wiley, Quality Assurance Manager
MacMillan Bloedel

"Here is an approach to focus on leadership and corporate culture change that is just as practical for a university setting as it is for other service or manufacturing environments. Change must occur from the top down and is illustrated in this book."

John Elizandro, Vice President
Institutional Advancement, Villanova University

"The corporate world knows that change is difficult. Larry is offering a continuous improvement process which addresses the very fiber of that resistance— leadership behavior."

Bob Davenport, Ph.D., Director of Technical Services
DuCoa, a DuPont/ConAgra Company

"*Frustration Is Your Organization's Best Friend* pulls together a description of the process and the fundamental behavioral issues that are relevant to a good management environment. After personally experiencing Dr. Cole's process at work, it's a good reminder of the importance of the lessons learned and of the importance of continued TWMS implementation."

Chris Long, President
Florida Drum Company

"Corporations can be profitable without this, but this is for companies who want to reach their maximum potential by enhancing the quality of life environment for their people."

Ted Gammill, CEO
K.W. Bancshares, Inc.

"Most companies don't fail for lack of talent or a strategic plan. Too often management fails to follow that plan and drops back to their comfort zone. This book has the answers about organizational change that so many managers have overlooked. Frustration can lead to success by improving working relationships and teamwork. This book shows how it's done."

Terry Reynolds, Vice President of Human Resources
Arrow Automotive Industries

FRUSTRATION IS YOUR ORGANIZATION'S BEST FRIEND

Measuring Corporate Culture Change

Larry Cole, Ph.D.

LifeSkills Publishers
5 Towering Pines
Conway, AR 72032

Although the author and publisher have made every effort to ensure the accuracy and completeness of information contained in this book, we assume no responsibility for errors, inaccuracies, omissions, or any inconsistency herein. Any slights of people, places, or organizations are unintentional.

First printing 1996

ISBN 1-888134-00-3

LCCN 95-071928

Editing, design, typesetting, and printing services provided by About Books, Inc., 425 Cedar Street, Buena Vista, CO 81211, (800) 548-1876.

ATTENTION CORPORATIONS, UNIVERSITIES, COLLEGES, AND PROFESSIONAL ORGANIZA-TIONS: Quantity discounts are available on bulk purchases of this book for educational or training purposes. Special books or book excerpts can also be created to fit specific needs. For information, please contact LifeSkills Publishers, 5 Towering Pines, Conway, AR 72032 or call (501) 327-1728.

❖ *Acknowledgments* ❖

I must first recognize the countless number of supervisors who have served as my teachers by sharing their knowledge and frustrations with me. These teachers taught me well and I owe them a debt of gratitude. Thank you for helping this student.

I also want to thank the organizations who took a chance to implement a rather unique process to improve their corporate culture and the CEOs who led the successful change efforts. You are the ones who are most responsible for this book.

I also want to recognize Jack Kanak, Ph.D., who served as my advisor and mentor in graduate school at the University of Oklahoma. He took a chance on a naive graduate student and gave me opportunities to teach, conduct research and publish in scientific journals that provided the basic tools for my adult career.

My appreciation goes to Sonja Keith for her constructive editorial suggestions, and to Doris King for making certain that everything else was done so I could spend time on writing. Marilyn Ross with About Books, Inc. deserves special recognition for transforming the manuscript into the book you are reading. Her professional advice was an invaluable resource. Last, and certainly not

least is my wife, Shelvie—who understands I am not a
workaholic, just someone who has a lot to do!

❖ *Table of Contents* ❖

❖ *Introduction* ❖

Only 30 percent of the companies implementing a major change effort such as total quality improvement or reengineering are successful. This pitiful success rate is in spite of the fact that change is imperative to maintain a competitive posture in this fast-paced, changing world. This failure rate can't be attributed to available information. The market is flooded with books dealing with quality improvement, reengineering and implementing organization change. With the abundance of information available, and the well-known fact that an organization must change or get left behind the pack, one could make the logical conclusion the change success rate is 80 to 90 percent. But that's not the way it is.

We've got to accept the challenge to do better!

Since *people* implement change and not organizations, the logical conclusion is that 70 percent of the people are not changing. Most of the energy to date has been focused on the tools of change (teams, statistical process control, reengineering and other process improvement procedures), while the people side of the change formula has received lip service at best. The irony of it all is that people will ultimately determine success. Considering this fact, one might wonder why the change efforts have not begun with the people. Could the reason be that working with the technical side of change is easier than the people side? Or has the assumption been made that people will automatically change to support the technical changes? Whatever the reason, the challenge of working to change people has to be accepted.

The people side of an organization is referred to as the "corporate culture," the way we do things around here. So we are really talking about changing the organization's corporate culture. If the corporate culture does not support organizational change, it will not happen.

Perhaps one of the more vivid illustrations is the clash that occurs when the autocratic, "do as I tell you," corporate culture style talks about implementing a change effort to increase employee participation. Just how much success do you think will be achieved if this company implements a customer service process to delegate decision making closer to the customer? It is doomed for failure because the change effort contradicts the corporate culture.

Based on my experiences working with organizations, there are four corporate culture categories:

1. Those who remain focused on the change effort

2. Those who talk more than they act

3. Those who actively work to remain dysfunctional

4. Those who are dead and, most likely, don't know it

Which one person has the most impact upon the organization's corporate culture? You're right. It's the CEO. In our illustration, the CEO has to begin the process of delegating decisions closer to the customer. If not, the *I'll believe it when I see it* organizational disease will strangle the change effort. Whether we like it or not, direct reports at every level are looking up as high as possible to see if the up-line management structure is walking the talk of change—or simply mouthing the words. And as usual, actions speak louder than words.

Introduction

Whether we like it or not, *change must occur from the top down.* The CEO begins the change process and holds the management structure accountable to cascade it throughout the organization. These are the two primary responsibilities of the CEO when implementing change. Never does the CEO rid him or herself of the responsibility of leading the change effort.

Frustration Is Your Organization's Best Friend was written to show you a structured data-based decision making process to change an organization's corporate culture. The change effort begins with the CEO and involves virtually everyone in the organization. The process outlined in this book has the capability of measuring the degree the CEO, as well as other members of the management team, changes to implement the desired corporate culture.

It's important for you to know the process is not a theoretical one. You will read actual data generated by working with organizations. As you read this book, you will see the advocated process is founded on the following principles:

CEO-led change effort

Data-based to measure progress

Practical and easily implemented

Accountable in all areas

The process offers every team member the opportunity for continuous improvement. I guarantee this process will work for you, if you will work the process! Obviously I can't guarantee that you will do that, only you can make that decision.

Now let's read and learn about a unique process that can provide the structure for both individual and corporate culture change. It leads to the successful implementation of other organizational change efforts as well.

Something to Remember When Working with Change

When nothing seems to help, I go and look at a stone-cutter hammering away at his rock perhaps a hundred times without as much as a crack showing in it. Yet, at the hundred and first blow it will split in two and I know it was not that blow that did it, but all that had gone before.

Jacob Riss

❖1❖

Making Frustration Your Organization's Best Friend

What You Will Learn

When you finish this chapter, you will understand the importance of creating frustration.

Your Organization's Best Friend?

Frustration! I can almost hear you question my sanity: "How can anything so uncomfortable be a friend?" But before you judge me to be crazy—or worse, before you decide to quit reading this book, do us both a favor and answer the following questions:

1. Do you want your organization to be mediocre?
2. Do you want your organization to be complacent?
3. Do you want your organization to be average?

My guess is your answers are not only "No," but "Heck No!"

You probably find even the remote possibility that your organization would be characterized by any of these questions to be downright repulsive. I don't mean to hurt your feelings, but your organization may be more characteristic of these three questions than you think. The comfort of what you are doing right now can be a vicious trap leading to the premature death of your organization.

I can almost hear you again. This time you're saying, "By gosh, my organization isn't going to die prematurely!" But the history of corporate America is filled with those who have remained locked in their comfort zone, blindly watching their organizations die a slow, albeit painless, death.

Remember the proverbial frog story? Place a frog in a pot of hot water and what will the frog do? It jumps out to escape the pain, of course. But place that same frog in a pot of cold water and begin warming it ever so slowly. What will the frog do this time? It becomes acclimated to the water, ignoring the rising temperature until it is too late. The frog, comfortable to the end, dies.

You've got to remember, if you've been swimming in the halls of your organization for quite some time, the temperature may be reaching the death point and you may not be aware of it. Sounds impossible? Well let me ask you a couple more questions.

1. Have you ever been frustrated?
2. Did you like it?

Now do you see the problem? All of us have been frustrated and "no" we did not like it. Frustration is uncomfortable, so we tend to avoid it. But avoiding what is uncomfortable can lock us in our comfort zone.

Time for a New Paradigm

It is time for a paradigm shift. We've got to become dissatisfied with what we have, before we will even consider a change effort. Therefore, frustration is the fuel for change. It's our best friend. It's the energy which pushes us out of the comfort zone. Without it, we run the risk of becoming average, complacent and mediocre. As painful as this frustration is, it's the initial fire to ignite the desire to change.

If I asked you to list the strengths of your organization, you could do so. You could also list the weaknesses. Operationally speaking, these are within your organization's comfort zone. There is no question that you could improve the weaknesses, and you probably could improve the strengths. In doing so you're going to create a difference between where you are and what you want to improve. I call this difference the gap of frustration.

Leaders who are successfully taking an organization through the minefield of change look frustration right in the eyes. They realize the importance of using frustration to bring about organizational change. Consequently, these leaders create frustration.

Let's look at an example provided by our space shuttle missions and see how it applies to change.

The space shuttle uses more fuel in the first three feet of its flight than it uses the remainder of the trip. In other words, a great amount of energy is required to lift off and leave the launching pad, or comfort zone.

We would like to think that most organizations begin change from a dead stop, but that's not true. We must actually overcome those active forces pulling the opposite direction, against change, as we listen to the battle cry that "organizational change is difficult" or "we don't need to change" ringing through the halls. This is like the space shuttle not just sitting on the launch pad, but the launch pad actually pulling the space shuttle down toward the earth's center as hard as it could. That would be an interesting sight, wouldn't it?

Leaders know it takes a great deal of frustration to overcome the active resistance and dead weight of an organization. They accept the challenge to identify the sources of frustration and make certain everyone else in the organization understands this frustration as well. Such leaders organize communication campaigns and internal marketing strategies to show everyone the disadvantages and pitfalls of the present situation. As people become dissatisfied with the present situation, the frustration intensifies. That's good. You want to increase the frustration to the boiling point quickly enough so the frog will jump out.

Perhaps we need to begin thinking *"organizational change is easy!"* This battle cry sends chills down the corporate halls. You are not going to be fooled are you? Too many people have told you that it is hard and, of course, you have your own failed attempts to prove it. So the challenge is to "make *change* easier." Frustration helps make change easier!

Every writer and consultant is preaching, "be on the cutting edge of change." Or as Joel Barker depicts, be the pioneer leading your organization on an untested and uncharted journey. Be out front. Be ahead of your competition. Be the pacesetter. Let others play catch up.

All of that sounds good, exciting and challenging. And you probably want to think such terms characterize your organization. Rest assured, however, that being a pacesetter requires that you welcome frustration. *Frustration becomes your best friend.*

As your friend, you must not only be willing to look for frustration, but welcome it with open arms. Yes, you can learn to enjoy the pain of frustration, once you understand it is a positive signal that your organization is alive and wanting to grow.

In Summary

Being dissatisfied with what we have is the prerequisite for change. It is the energy source that pushes us to change. I call this dissatisfaction "frustration." Without it we remain as we are. In this fast-paced, changing world that means becoming complacent, average and mediocre.

Our new lifestyle is to create frustration so we can constantly be changing, growing and improving.

> *The enjoyment of the uncomfortable is just another ironic characteristic of organizational life.*

❖2❖

Fear and Confusion Are Friends of Change

What You Will Learn

Learning *how to manage change* is the key ingredient. This chapter will discuss how to implement change and manage the energy sources that facilitate the change process.

The Death Cycle

The death cycle is usually the same. Someone has a great idea!!! The CEO or other high ranking staff members decide "this is what we shall become!" So we spend a zillion dollars in time and other resources figuring out how this new fangdangled creation is going to work in our organization. We spend another small fortune buying books, sending people to seminars, benchmarking other organizations and purchasing audio tapes, video tapes and work books until they ooze from every nook, cranny and shelf.

I often find books and videos stored on shelves in corporate halls. Employees never knew these products existed. My bet is you can find the same in your organization.

Now comes the big day. It is time to announce the new organization. Today we are creating a new tomorrow. Everyone has the new vision and they are clamoring to get on board the train that will take them on a certain journey to success. We are champing at the bit and can't wait to reap the benefits of this new idea.

So we begin with excitement and enthusiasm flowing down the halls, dripping off the pictures, scurrying in every direction. It's part of every sentence spoken. You would swear some higher power or spiritual endeavor has taken over the place. Perhaps something has been added to the drinking water or to the air we breathe. No doubt, there is something different going on today.

Then it happens. As the new tomorrow is being created, it continues to run smack-dab into the old yesterdays—and all the associated paradigms. I have listed some of my favorite ones below. You can probably add a few to the list.

- That will never work around here.
- We don't do that here.
- We've been doing it this way for as long as I can remember, so why would we change now?
- I'm not doing anything differently, I don't care what those over-educated smart alecks say.
- Nobody cooperates around here.
- I'm supposed to do what? Why hasn't anyone told me?
- Recommending something around here is like putting it in a black hole.

- Put it in this file and we will get to it later.
- I'll believe it when I see it.

All this old emotional baggage begins to take its toll. After some time, people talk less about the new tomorrow. They begin to attend meetings without being prepared; to make matters worse, there is no embarrassment about the lack of preparedness. The embarrassed ones are those who did prepare, because they stand out like a sore thumb while their peers and colleagues wonder silently (and sometimes out loud), "Why did that fool spend all that wasted time for nothing?"

Next, meetings scheduled to work on the continued process begin to get canceled because another operational fire is roaring out of control. Damage control continues to be the name of the game, thus we better bring in the water brigade.

Life drains from the once strong, vibrant, enthusiastic body. The tumor of resistance has now become a growing cancer. The new tomorrow is being prepared for the last rites, which people forget to attend because some fool scheduled it during the lunch hour. The gall to think that anyone would waste their lunch hour attending such a stupid ceremony when we knew it was going to die from the beginning.

Learned helplessness wins again! The new paradigm of change got beat up so badly by the paradigms of old that the change effort died.

"Learned helplessness" means giving up. Psychologist William Seligman found that dogs confronted with an inescapable shock often just gave up and did nothing to resist the pain.

It appears that learned helplessness is a disease of epidemic proportions that instinctively attacks organizational change. People just get tired of beating their heads against a brick wall and quit doing so to avoid the pain.

But I haven't told you anything you don't already know about organizational change. The new processes, called Total Quality Management and Process Reengineering, were supposed to be different, so invigorating as to awaken the sleeping dinosaurs crowding the organization's halls.

Quality Rigor Mortis Paradigm

The American total quality management revolution was begun with a new zeal and zest for living. "We have found the way" thanks to Deming, Juran, Crosby and other quality gurus. Organizations everywhere began clamoring to initiate quality improvement efforts that promised to make the company more competitive in the new global economy. The old syndrome, "everyone is doing it so our company better do it also" began running rampant throughout organizational circles.

Consultants waving quality improvement flags jumped out of every crevice singing the same song, "Hire me and together we'll solve your problems and get you back on track." All the books and organizational songs and dances had to include the words "total quality management," or "quality improvement process," or "continuous quality improvement," or "total quality improvement" to draw someone's attention to it. Words became a marketing tool and total quality management became another package wrapper.

The new process was ushered in as the savior that would pull American industries out of the quality doldrums. It was a well-known fact that Japanese businesses and industries were beating the socks off of their American counterparts who had become fat, sassy and arrogant in their comfort zones.

Consumers with money in their pockets and wanting more for their money followed the quality trail and bought Japanese products, much to the dismay of American industries who wondered, "How could the American public betray us like that?" Actually it was quite easy, since the American industries betrayed their customers first. Here is an example of the old truism, "you receive what you share with others" and those who shared first were complaining about it.

After the quality improvement process came into being, the media was full of success stories with the central theme, "Yes, after just five months our organization has trimmed costs by a zillion dollars and profits have risen beyond our wildest expectations. Everyone is happy and prospective employees are beating down our doors to gain entry into our ivory towers."

During this new era we did not hear much about anyone having difficulty implementing this process. It was easy. Simply put your people through hours of training, create quality improvement teams, assign a facilitator and a quality guru to assist each team, and have these teams report to a quality council who may or may not have the authority to act upon the recommendations without the blessings from the higher management power.

Then reality begins to set in. This gush of success stories slows to a trickle. The gusher is now spurting research suggesting that some 70 percent of the efforts to initiate the quality improvement process die the slow and painful death previously described. People are shaking their heads and wondering why. "How could such a good idea die such a premature death?" Unfortunately, the news about "death to quality improvement processes" is spreading yet another paradigm: "the quality rigor mortis paradigm."

The pessimists are having a heyday with this quality improvement bandwagon. "See, another idea for *the idea of the month* graveyard. I knew if I just waited around long enough and did nothing, this too would pass. After all, our organization has a reputation for talking about change, trying to change, but never changing."

It's a shame we are spreading such a paradigm. Think about it for a moment. If everyone believed it, where would we be? We would expect to fail without having tried—thus, we would never even try. Learned helplessness is a terrible disease, wouldn't you agree?

But did you know that not all of Seligman's dogs gave up? About one-third of them continued searching for ways to improve the situation even though it was impossible. I am sure the dogs suffering from learned helplessness criticized those optimistic fools for wasting energy in much the same way that our business and industry skeptics are saying, "I told them not to waste any money on such a foolish project!"

So if 70 percent of the efforts to implement quality improvement processes fail, that means 30 percent are successful! Now all we have to do is to figure out a way to be part of that 30 percent. What these numbers are telling us is that we're facing the challenge and opportunity to find a better way to implement quality improvement changes in our organizations. We can do that!

Don't you find it interesting that about 30 percent of the dogs continued searching for a way to stop the endless shocks . . . and about 30 percent of organizations successfully implement quality improvement change. I wonder if dogs and these corporate leaders have something in common?

Leaders who successfully initiate change know that frustration is their friend. It serves as the electrical shock that keeps them jumping, searching for a better way. There is no resting, because the only way to avoid the pain of frustration is to find that better way. And that way does not include sticking our head in the sand like an ostrich, closing our eyes and pretending to be blind so we don't see it. These leaders know that learned helplessness creates constant pain and creates an organization with poor self-esteem that is depressed, without energy and *dead.*

Better Know Where You Want to Go to Get There

In the process of finding a better way, these same leaders realize the importance of creating a clear vision of where they want to go. The vision needs to be as crystal clear as possible because it is the energy source that pulls you out of your organization's comfort zone. I will show you momentarily how this energy source works in concert with frustration, but first there is a point that needs to be made. Let me ask you two questions that speak to this point.

1. Did you know where you were going this morning when you left you house to go to work?

2. Did you get there?

Simple questions which illustrate a very important but often forgotten principle: *To get where you want to go, you must know where you want to go.* Equally important, *you must know the point from which you begin.*

Have you ever thought about how difficult it would be to get to somewhere traveling in your car if you didn't know where you were going? Nor can you get where you want to go, if you do not know the point from which you begin. Isn't it amazing how we take such simple, and yet important, truisms for granted?

To explain the powerful energy source of knowing where you want to go, consider the last time you purchased an item that exceeded your budget. As you were looking at it, touching it and possibly even using it, it kept screaming, "buy me, buy me, buy me." Finally the energy source was too great. You just had to buy it to reduce the tension.

Now you've reduced one set of tension and created a new set. The new screaming thought is, "How am I going to pay for this?" Most of the time, we think of ways to pay for the purchased item within our budget to reduce the tension. I'll explain why this is true in just a moment.

Organizational change operates on the same principle. Defining success in clear terms so employees realize the benefits of the change serves as a magnetic force to create a positive energy source to move the organization forward.

The Law of Closure

These changes to reduce tension illustrate a very important principle called the Law of Closure. Operationally defined, the Law of Closure means we work to reduce tensions, thereby creating a state of balance. For some reason, few authors and consultants discussing organizational change mention this very powerful and important principle.

For example, physical tension is created when we're hungry, thirsty or tired. So what do we do? We do whatever is necessary to reduce the tension and return to a balanced state, commonly referred to as homeostasis or equilibrium. Now you know why you were able to not only buy, but also pay for, the expensive purchase.

And there are more examples. Tension is created when we cut ourselves and bleed. The blood, however, has a coagulant to stop the bleeding and begin the process of reducing the tension. With time, the wound closes and eventually heals (assuming we don't continue cutting at it), returning to a state of balance.

Another example is one you may have forgotten. We should have two black holes in our perceptual field, because there is a hole in the retina through which the optic nerves pass to the brain. Thus, part of our perceptual images fall on the portion of the retina which is void of rods or cones. One can't see without these receptors so we should see two holes in our perceptual fields. But do you see them? No, because the brain closes the picture to present a complete image of balance.

This phenomenon can be demonstrated by looking at the following illustrations.

Finding Your Blind Spot

1. Close your right eye and stare at the cross. Hold the page about a foot from your eye. Move the page until the star falls on your blind spot and disappears.

2. Close your right eye and stare at the cross. Hold the page about a foot from your left eye and move the page until the break in the line falls on your blind spot. The line will look unbroken.

Figure 1

The Law of Closure is a natural law. It's operating all the time to help us remain in balance. When dealing with personal or organizational change, the Law of Closure helps us remain in balance by reducing tension. First is the frustration created by the dissatisfaction with the comfort zone (which we discussed in Chapter One). Second is the tension associated when defining a clear vision of what we want to happen. Now we have a specifically defined gap of frustration between where we are and where we want to go. Creating these tensions can actually help to propel the organization down the change journey as we work to reduce the tension (i.e. Law of Closure.)

Figure two illustrates the two energy sources encouraging change: frustration pushing us out of the comfort zone and the pull created by wanting where it is we're going.

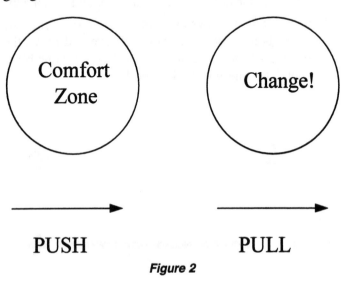

PUSH   **PULL**

Figure 2

If these were the only two energy sources operating, organizational change would be easy. But we know the old paradigms continue to operate in our corporate culture, so we know better, right?

As the organization begins to step out of its comfort zone, it runs smack-dab into these old paradigms we discussed earlier. Now, added to all those old dinosaur paradigms is the fact that we don't know if the change will be successful (the crystal ball becomes clouded). When that happens, fear begins to strike at the very fiber of our existence.

At these times we forget that fear is really an acronym:

Find
Every
Available
Resource

Actually, we don't like fear any better (perhaps even less) than we did frustration, so we have a tendency to run back to our comfort zone in accordance to the Law of Closure. After all, we do not keep our hand in boiling water, do we? An automatic response takes over: we pull our hand out without even thinking about it. This same autonomic response system encourages us to run away from the pain of fear to keep from damaging our bodies, just as the frog also jumps out when placed in a pan of hot water.

And there's more! Change is more difficult than we originally imagined. Creating a quality mind-set is more than posting charts on the walls and assigning quality improvement teams. Change is something we must do all day, every single day. To quit smoking, we must quit every day, not every other day. This is a difficult pill to swallow. The difficulty associated with changes offers a temptation to start shouting, "Whose crazy idea was this change anyway?"

And there's more yet! There are the frustrations associated with mistakes and failures. All the glorious benefits of change that pulled us out of the comfort zone seem to never appear on the horizon. Consequently, people become frustrated, disheartened and question whether this is going to work.

The organization is at a very crucial point. The fear, hard work and seeming disillusionment encourages one to begin thinking about aborting the change process and returning to the comfort zone. The ease of the comfort zone appears to be screaming, "Don't be so stupid. Come back to the comfort zone!" Yes, the Law of Closure can also serve as an enemy in the change process as going back may be less painful than continuing the change.

With two energy sources encouraging us to change, and others encouraging us to remain the same, the organization becomes confused. "What do we do now?" becomes the battle cry. Again, confusion is not a lot of fun so it seems only logical to run back to the comfort zone to escape from this pain. Here's the Law of Closure again!

We tend to forget that fear and confusion are natural signals that we are in the process of change. These are nothing to worry about. As a matter of fact, we should enjoy experiencing them . . . we are changing, which is what we want to happen! OOPS! Another paradigm shift—fear and confusion are friends.

Figure three illustrates the resistance to change created by fear and confusion.

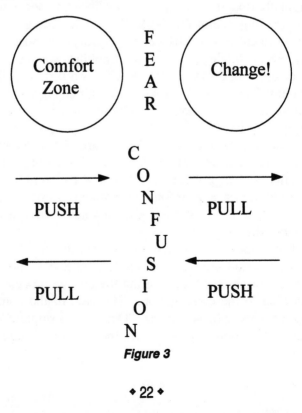

Figure 3

Would You Rather Be a Turtle or a Squirrel?

I often use the analogy of a squirrel and a turtle to illustrate the change process. What is the first thing a turtle does as it starts to walk across the road? You're right, stick its neck out of its shell. You've never seen a turtle walking across the road with its neck tucked in its shell have you? What's the first thing it does when it senses danger during this journey? It stops and withdraws its head. After the danger-inducing situation has passed, the head pops back out and the turtle continues its journey.

Do you know anyone who purposefully tries to run over a turtle crossing the road? Probably not. Most of us want the turtle to successfully complete its journey. You probably know people who have even stopped and helped one cross the road.

Now let's compare the turtle's journey with that of a squirrel. The squirrel knows that it is fast, so it waits beside the road. It sees the oncoming automobile, but it waits. Finally, it decides the timing is right and darts out into the road. When it gets out there, it quickly decides that it has underestimated the speed of the automobile and overestimated its own speed. Sadly realizing its mistake—it stops—turns around—and takes off again.

Not ever having had a time management course, the squirrel fails to realize that valuable seconds are consumed in all this stopping, turning and starting. As it runs back to its comfort zone, it often gets struck by the automobile. But again, do you know anyone who tries to hit squirrels on the road? Probably not. Yet when it experienced fear, it had to run back to its comfort zone.

Many organizations act like a squirrel and retreat to their comfort zone when they should be more like the turtle and take their comfort zone with them on the journey. It is easier to be a turtle when we understand the forces that facilitate, as well as interfere with, change. To manage change we must:

- Become frustrated by identifying what can be improved.

- Define success. What do you want to become?

- Use frustration to begin the change process, but immediately focus on what you want to become. Let where you are going be your guiding light.

- Remember that the resistance offered by not knowing what will happen, the hard work required to change, and the temptation to quit brought on by confusion can all be overcome by persistently taking steps toward your goal.

- Keep on keeping on and recognize all successes.

Sometimes the speed of change seems to occur at a snail's pace. But remember that speed is relative, as evidenced by the snail that was run over by a turtle. While in the emergency room, the doctor asked the snail if he knew what happened. The snail replied, "No, it happened so quickly!"

There is nothing magical or mystical about managing change, you just simply keep managing it. Learning how to manage it is the key difference between those who successfully implement change and those who do not. It is a matter of persistence, of maintaining the necessary confidence level. You must know your change effort will be successful. Keep on doing the right things right during moments of uncertainty. Confusion, fear, mistakes and perceived failures are all positive signs that change is being implemented in your organization. OOPS! There's that paradigm shift again.

In Summary

There is a cartoon caption that reads, *"People want to go to heaven, but they don't want to die first,"* which also characterizes the change process. Change produces a considerable amount of fear of the unknown and confusion when the pushes and pulls of the comfort zone begin to grip at our emotions. The uncomfortableness of these emotions encourages us to take the path of least resistance and quit.

Successful change agents understand that fear and confusion are really friends signaling that change is occurring as desired. During such times, it is imperative to maintain the focus of the desired outcome and use the Law of Closure to continue propelling the change effort.

It's difficult to remember that frustration,

fear and confusion are your friends while you

are being bruised by the process of change.

But when you remember,

they become powerful allies.

❖3❖

Change Begins with Me

What You Will Learn

Senior managers often talk the talk of change, but they don't walk it. The commitment to change and the implementation of change must both begin at the top.

Change from the Top Down or Bottom Up?

You've seen and heard before what I am about to tell you. The senior management issues a dictate that the organization is embarking upon a new quality improvement program or other major change effort, then the organization initiates a flurry of activity to implement the program. Of course this dictate is important, because the commitment for change must come from the top of the organizational structure. If top management is not committed, there won't be any change.

Unfortunately, the commitment letter is where the involvement of some top managers stops. They feel as though their work is completed once the memorandum is distributed.

When senior management's work ends with this memo, the organization is operating under the assumption that the change is for someone else. This someone else is usually lower levels of management and hourly employees. The problem with this approach is that organizations are usually riddled with the *"I'll believe it when I see it"* disease. Lower management levels and hourly employees are waiting to see the up-line managers make all of these miraculous changes. They, on the other hand, are waiting on the lower management levels and the hourly employees to change. Obviously, if the change is always for someone else, there won't be much.

Too frequently, implementing quality improvement processes suffers from the "someone else will change" disease. Up-line managers forget about the "I'll believe it when I see it" disease, which then gives credence to the old and true cliché, "You must talk the talk and walk the walk."

Managers will readily admit the importance of providing a role model for the organization, but saying and doing are two different behaviors. The importance of *doing* is often forgotten. The irony of the situation is: in times of change, leading by example becomes even more important. Let's address management's very special role.

Managers Walking and Talking Change

Talking the talk of change occurs at both the formal and informal levels. At the formal level, it means placing the change process at the top of the corporate agenda. To do so, the following should be considered:

- Why it's imperative for the organization to change; i.e., intensify the frustration with the present comfort zone.

- Decide and discuss the vision of the change process. This helps everyone see the new comfort zone.

- Ensure employee involvement in the change process.

- Monitor and publish progress.
- Hold people accountable for change.

A planned procedure for such formal discussions sends the message that the organization is serious about successfully implementing the changes.

At the informal level, senior management needs to continue discussing the same agenda to help everyone understand the need for change. All participants should see the new vision. Managers can keep their fingers on the pulse of the organization by soliciting input and feedback from employees at all levels. These conversations can occur in the break room, lunch room, in the halls and even the infamous meeting room formally known as the restroom.

The bottom line is the CEO and other managers need to be seen and heard participating in the events that promote the change agenda.

Individuals in the management structure need to have a plan to change their personal habits to support the corporate change agenda. Letting others know about this plan and keeping them posted as to the progress being made is a powerful message.

There Is More, Much More

An often ill-fated methodology employed by many organizations is the proud display of their statistical process control charts or progress made by quality improvement teams as testimonies to the success of their change process. Don't take me wrong. Both of these are integral parts of a quality improvement process, but there is more, much more.

Both statistical process control charts and quality improvement teams are tools, just as the computer and word processing software I am using to write this book are tools. The keys I push or the words typed on the screen are not writing. These are only signs of writing.

Writing is more than simply pushing keys. Writing occurs in the head.

Unfortunately, many attempts to implement quality improvement focus on the use of tools. Street talk is rich with examples of organizations implementing quality improvement teams whose recommendations fall on deaf ears or die a slow death in the hierarchy, waiting to be acted upon. Employees create beautiful statistical process control charts without fully realizing how to use them or failing to use them correctly after their completion.

Quality improvement must become more than the utilized tools. It must occur in the head. It must become a mind-set. Something that is done every day, all day long—not just when employees participate in a quality improvement team meeting or use the statistical process control chart. It must become an integral part of your infrastructure and corporate culture.

Is the Infrastructure an Enemy or a Friend?

Your organization's infrastructure consists of the lines of authority, natural work teams (departments) and the way you treat each other on a daily basis. This is your corporate culture. Whether you like it or not, your infrastructure can help you implement quality improvement processes—or be an additional source of interference. And for this reason, your infrastructure needs to be at the heart of your quality improvement change process.

The corporate culture can kill a good idea before its germination. For example, I'm reminded of an organization that asked me to help it develop a quality improvement process for their customer service program. Senior level managers told me they wanted to invert the pyramid to get decision making closer to the customer. After completing a diagnostic process to learn more about the organization, I met with the CEO and the committee responsible for customer service development.

In my report, I noted employees perceive decision making to be closely held among the higher levels of management. The CEO who was sitting at the end of his long wooden conference table in the infamous power position looked up at me at that point and said, "That's correct, Larry. I do make most of the decisions and that won't change!" Excuse me! Does this philosophy seem a bit inconsistent with inverting the organizational pyramid?

Another observation was that the management staff in general, and the senior managers in particular, were not very friendly. Most of the time, these managers didn't even speak to their staff. Again, the CEO looked up at me and said, "That's right again. I often walk the halls and don't speak to employees and that's not going to change either!"

My recommendation to that committee was to forget about inverting the organizational pyramid until they were ready to lead the change effort. If the senior managers are not going to change, you can rest assured the effort will soon belong to their idea of the month graveyard.

When the corporate culture doesn't kill the quality improvement change process, it can seriously injure it.

An example of such maiming is a company which had three quality instructors training the 1000+ employee base. Their first attempt was to put together about 60 quality improvement teams throughout the organization. These teams generated a multitude of recommendations for improvement. Then they hit the infrastructure.

The CEO had about 10 direct reports who used the "circle the wagon" leadership style. Not only was there little cooperation, but often times there was all-out war. The CEO did not like conflict. Instead of working to resolve it, he perpetuated it by ignoring it until the blood began to flow. Then he would write one of his infamous edicts . . . "They shall not fight." You can imagine the fate of the recommendations of these 60 quality improvement teams.

The second attempt to implement quality improvement in this organization included fewer quality improvement teams consisting of front-line supervisors and employees. (By the way, this plant was operating under a corporate dictate to implement quality improvement processes.) These teams only worked with issues that could safely be handled by this level of management.

By ignoring up-line management, changes were made, although all agreed the potential for improvement will never be realized with the prevailing "circle the wagons" mentality of the senior managers.

A conservative definition of quality improvement through the use of teams technically qualifies this organization as having implemented quality improvement, but is it being incorporated into the corporate culture? No. The two-tiered quality improvement system in this organization is sabotaging the ultimate success of the process.

There are times when the CEO bestows blessing on the quality improvement process, but for a variety of reasons does not wish to participate. Again, the organization struggles, but some progress can be made. Quite frankly, some may wonder if the improvement is worth the pain in these instances. I may be in the minority, but any lasting improvement is worth the pain in my opinion.

For example, one organization focused on the middle and front-line management levels to improve the quality of the working relationships between departments. The CEO washed his hands of the process by announcing he was delegating this to his direct reports. You can imagine the initial attitude of these managers. "Why should we do this when the CEO won't do it?" was the beginning battle cry. Fortunately, the staff was able to quit shooting themselves in their feet with this motto and worked to understand the needs of their internal customers.

The major obstacle we were not able to overcome in this organization was interference by the senior managers. One senior manager was really obstinate and did not encourage his staff to participate. Whenever our attempts to improve the working relationship crossed over into this line of supervision, the effort usually achieved very little progress. Sometimes we would get good lip service about cooperating, but action usually failed to follow the words. Without any accountability system to encourage change, it was a difficult situation. In spite of all of this resistance, a strong nucleus of managers achieved progress.

Another CEO excused himself from participating in the process by telling his staff, "Whatever you want to do is fine with me." So the process began.

In this instance, there was a line of supervision which was not cooperative. To make matters worse, the CEO chose not to hold the manager accountable for cooperating with the process. Even without CEO support, this organization was able to improve its infrastructure and design a process to implement quality improvement processes.

I say all of this to let you know that progress can be made without active support from the CEO. Some people will attempt to tell you that progress can not be made in such instances, but these examples support a different conclusion. However, the handicap of their absence is usually such an obstacle that the organization rarely achieves its full potential.

These case histories may initially seem inconsistent with the major theme of this chapter, change starting at the top and working down. But they are consistent with that theme. The commitment came from senior managers to implement changes. These organizations did not, however, achieve their potential because the CEOs were not directly involved.

Let's finish this chapter on a more successful note and provide a couple of examples in which CEO-led change produced significant results.

I worked with an organization under a corporate dictate to begin a quality improvement process. The corporate quality instructor was scheduled into the organization within the year to implement the process. The CEO realized the organization was not ready for this change. He had department managers fighting each other and some of them were even disgruntled at him.

I certainly was not welcomed with open arms into this organization. The word "consultant" was not a kind name. Several months earlier, another consultant had spent time showing videos and leading boring discussions. That was the performance level several expected from another consultant. Consequently, several managers initially despised participating in team building processes.

The CEO demonstrated strong leadership and required management staff to participate. Not only did the managers complete the team building process, but they enjoyed doing it. A sure sign of success occurred when several of the original indignant managers were so encouraged about the progress made that they asked for the consulting relationship to continue. This staff did a remarkable job staying focused. The CEO was great. He made certain that every assignment was completed as scheduled. Prognosis is that this organization will continue to achieve higher levels of improvement.

Let's look at one more example to illustrate the success that can be achieved when both the commitment and the change start at the top. This organization had originally spent considerable financial resources training its entire employee base on quality improvement processes, tools and teams. Several quality improvement teams were established and made recommendations to the senior managers. The senior managers weren't ready to participate in the process and the recommendations fell on deaf ears. Consequently, the project died.

A new plant manager wanted to resurrect the quality improvement process. You can imagine the outcry! Most of the employee base and managers expected this effort to fail also. Passive resistance was a major epidemic.

The plant manager remained focused and optimistically accepted the setbacks with an attitude of "we'll do better next time." He kept chipping at the quality boulder with a hammer by completing assignments at the senior manager level and he held his staff accountable for the completion of the assignments down line.

Employees were finally believing. This is for real this time. The prognosis is excellent. Quality improvement is alive and will continue to be the walk in the halls of this company. Demonstrated change by the senior managers set the pace for change.

I Created What I Have

Managers often resist realizing that they gave birth to the existing corporate culture and attitudes toward change. Employees are going to respond to the examples provided by the leaders in the organization. If a manager is not willing to accept that truism, then that manager needs to be elsewhere.

If your organization is contemplating providing additional structure to its quality improvement process (I say that because you have quality processes in place whether you have a formal quality improvement process or not) or some other change, then by all means accept the reality that the management structure is the key to successfully implement the change. We would like all employees to be excited and willing participants in the change process demonstrating the attitude, *change begins with me*, but that won't occur while looking at discouraged, skeptical or pessimistic management faces.

You are reading about a process to manage change in your organization. If you are not willing to change, then perhaps you shouldn't continue reading this book. *And for Pete's sake, don't begin a change process if you are not willing to personally change and participate in this change process.* I say that without knowing your position in the organizational structure, because everyone in your organization will need to change.

In Summary

No one, but no one, can serve as a better antidote to the "I'll believe it when I see it" disease than an active CEO followed by a hyperactive management staff.

Conversely, remember that fish rot from the head down! Here's an interesting question: As a manager, am I going to be a rotting fish or a role model for change?

The decision I must make is to be

a friend of the change process, or its enemy.

❖4❖

The TeamWork Mission Statement

What You Will Learn

You will learn how to define an infrastructure and corporate culture that facilitates working together as a team. The TeamWork Mission Statement (TWMS) is the key to this process.

The TeamWork Mission Statement

The TeamWork Mission Statement describes how employees work together to achieve the corporate mission statement and the organization's business plan. Please note it is not a substitute for the corporate mission statement, nor does it address the business you're in, the organization's purpose or business objectives. Its sole purpose is to define how you want to work with each other while doing business. In other words, it is the official definition of your corporate culture, or how you do things in your organization.

You can also think of the TWMS as describing the lubrication for the working relationship between employees at all levels of the organization, horizontally as well as vertically. Consequently, the importance of this statement cannot be over emphasized.

Now, let's review a few examples.

Realizing each individual is a vital link in our organization, we honestly communicate, exhibit patience, respect and trust, acknowledge a job well done and cooperate toward our common goal.

❖ ❖ ❖

Employees working together with respect, caring, trust and honesty in order to communicate openly and provide quality care.

❖ ❖ ❖

To achieve our common goals, we are committed to TeamWork characterized by open communication, honesty, trust, respect and a positive mental attitude.

If your first reaction to reading these is that there is nothing particularly significant about any of them, then you have missed the point entirely. Reread these mission statements. Think about the words. These statements contain a list of values that drive the people side of the organization. Would you like to have an organization that could be characterized by any one of these statements? Name me one executive who would not!

Who Writes the TeamWork Mission Statement?

The TWMS is created by the employees (including management staff). A typical procedure is to work with several employee groups to create a working draft. Once the draft is completed, it can be distributed to all employees with instructions to further edit the statement.

Note the employee involvement procedure is a break in tradition in how most corporate mission statements are created. Most are written by a team of senior managers after which they are floated throughout the organization as its gospel. In reality, do you know the final resting place for most of these gospel statements? Correct. On walls, in brochures and other corporate publications. Can you recall your corporate mission statement? Most of the managers and employees I ask about their corporate mission statement, cannot tell me what it is, what it means or how it is used.

Unfortunately, the reality of most corporate mission statements is that they become expensive wall decorations. Employee involvement is the rule rather than the exception when creating the TWMS, for obvious reasons. Most employees do not like to be told what to do, but they do like to provide useful input. Being employee driven ensures "ownership." Plus it is the employees' statement as to how we are going to treat each other. The TWMS is to be a working document, not something taken lightly or simply hung on walls.

The challenge for management is to create an atmosphere in which the TWMS can flourish. In this respect, it is the manager's organizational prayer that needs to be recited daily as a reminder of how managers are to lead the organization on a moment-by-moment basis—every day, all day long.

In order for the TWMS to become an operational document, the statement endears another level of development. That is, employees operationally define the descriptive words in their TWMS to create *value statements*.

Let's use two previously listed TeamWork Mission Statements as examples of this process:

To achieve our common goals, we are committed to TeamWork characterized by open communication, honesty, trust, respect and a positive mental attitude.

This TWMS was further defined to include the following value statements:

Common Goals

1. We exceed our customer's expectations to provide a quality product.

Commitment

1. We are dedicated to the success of the company.

TeamWork

1. We understand each other's needs.
2. We willingly help each other succeed.
3. Problems are solved in a win/win manner.

Open Communication

1. We are encouraged to express our ideas.
2. We are kept informed.
3. We listen to facts before making a decision.

Honesty

1. We represent information accurately.
2. We look at situations objectively.

Trust

1. We do what we say we will do.
2. We work in a safe environment.

3. Managers support employees' decisions.

4. Confidential information is kept confidential.

Respect

1. All departments are considered equal.

2. We accept each other's ideas.

Positive Mental Attitude

1. We look for the good in everything.

2. We are friendly to each other.

3. We are courteous to each other.

These value statements provide the management structure clearer guidelines on "how to work with each other." Think of these value statements as a road map or a set of instructions. To further illustrate, let's look at one more example:

Employees working together with respect, caring, trust and honesty in order to communicate openly and provide quality care.

Working Together

1. We understand each other's needs.

2. We help each other to be successful.

3. We are working toward a common goal.

Respect

1. We listen to understand each other's point of view.

2. My supervisor uses my input in decision making.

3. Employees from the various departments are treated equally.

Caring

1. We are concerned about each other's feelings.

Trust

1. Confidential information is kept confidential.
2. My supervisor lets me do my job.
3. We do what we say we will do.

Honesty

1. We are told the truth.

Communicate Openly

1. We are encouraged to provide input.
2. We feel free to express ourselves without fear of retaliation.
3. We are kept informed.
4. We have the necessary information to do our job.

Quality Care

1. We exceed our patient's expectations.

Would you like to have an organization characterized by these definitions? Would such an organization be more prepared to implement quality improvement processes and other change efforts? You bet!

Measure, Measure, Measure

The next major step in this process is to quantify the TWMS to establish benchmark data and identify the organization's strengths and areas for improvement. The value statements are used to create a questionnaire and employees are asked to use an intensity scale to anonymously rate their company on each of these statements.

Employees are typically asked to rate the organization by using a seven-point scale ranging from 1 (Strongly Disagree) to 7 (Strongly Agree). Please note the means range from –3 (Strongly Disagree) to +3 (Strongly Agree) in our example. The data has been transformed by subtracting a 4 from each individual's score to create a

0 midpoint and to give 1 and 7 an equal weight of 3, 2 and 6 an equal weight of 2, and 3 and 5 an equal weight of 1. Number 4 becomes a 0. Thus the conversion is as follows:

Strongly Agree						Strongly Disagree
7	6	5	4	3	2	1
+3	+2	+1	0	−1	−2	−3

For illustrative purposes, let's use an example of a TWMS previously cited.

TeamWork Mission Statement

To achieve our common goals, we are committed to TeamWork characterized by open communication, honesty, trust, respect and a positive mental attitude.

Common Goals   **Mean**

1. We exceed our customers' expectations to provide a quality product.   +.60

Commitment

2. We are dedicated to the success of the company.   +.65

TeamWork

3. We understand each other's needs.   −1.06
4. We willingly help each other succeed.   −.98
5. Problems are solved in a win/win manner.   −1.32

Open Communication

6.	We are free to express our ideas.	−.71
7.	We are encouraged to express our ideas.	−.76
8.	We are kept informed.	−1.55
9.	We listen to the facts before making a decision.	−1.09

Honesty

10.	We represent information accurately.	−.65
11.	We look at situations objectively.	−.88

Trust

12.	We do what we say we will do.	−1.33
13.	We work in a safe environment.	−.98
14.	Managers support employees' decisions.	−1.16
15.	Confidential information is kept confidential.	−.53

Respect

16.	All departments are considered equal.	−1.68
17.	We accept each other's ideas.	−1.27

Positive Mental Attitude

18.	We look for the good in everything.	−1.14
19.	We are friendly to each other.	−.13
20.	We are courteous to each other.	−.40

Grand Mean   **−.82**

You can see these responses show a great deal of frustration in this organization. But if you are going to go anywhere, it is important to know the starting point. This benchmark data is the starting point. We will revisit benchmark data in Chapter 7 to illustrate the process to quantify corporate culture change.

Measuring the Supervisor

You probably already surmised that this procedure can also be used to rate supervisors and that is done when practical. As you can imagine, this procedure often causes some concern on the part of supervisors. Consequently, this procedure is often not used when collecting the benchmark data. When it can be implemented, there is an excellent opportunity to obtain information that will be extremely beneficial to supervisors and thus the organization. Let's look at an example when supervisors were rated along with the organization. (Company is the first column, Supervisor the second.)

TeamWork Mission Statement

We dedicate ourselves to reflect a positive mental attitude and treat each other with respect and equality as we cooperate an communicate openly to achieve the company's goals.

		Co. Mean	Sup. Mean
Positive Mental Attitude			
1.	We come to work happy.	1.18	.71
2.	We cheerfully complete jobs.	1.04	.57
3.	We are friendly to each other.	1.54	1.29
4.	We look for good/ accentuate the positive.	1.10	.57
5.	We think of each other as a friend.	1.22	.57
Respect			
6.	We are willing to do what we ask others to do.	1.43	.57
7.	Confidential information		

	is kept confidential.	1.35	–.71
8.	Constructive criticism is offered in private.	1.63	–.14

Equally

9.	Work is evenly distributed.	1.33	.71
10.	Rules and procedures are consistently applied.	1.10	.86
11.	We are trained on all procedures.	1.26	.43
12.	We are told the same information.	1.02	–.71
13.	Everyone is important regardless of position.	1.26	0.00

Cooperate

14.	We understand each other's needs.	1.32	.43
15.	We willingly help each other.	1.43	.43
16.	We are flexible enough to do whatever needs to be done.	1.31	.71
17.	Authority is delegated to do the job.	1.43	.57
18.	We do what we say we will do.	1.35	1.14
19.	We readily admit our mistakes.	.96	–.43

Communicate Openly

20.	We are free to express ideas.	1.96	1.14
21.	We are encouraged to express ideas.	1.78	.43
22.	We are listened to.	1.67	.71
23.	We are kept informed.	1.12	.43
24.	We receive pats on the back for a job well done.	1.52	–.29

Company's Goals

25.	These goals are defined.	1.22	.29
26.	These goals are communicated.	1.30	0.00
27.	Feedback is provided as to the progress in achieving these goals.	.90	−.29
28.	We are held accountable to achieve the goals.	1.59	−.14
	Grand Mean	**1.34**	**.37**

This organization clearly has less frustration than the previous example. You can also see that the supervisor's ratings did not mirror those of the company. But this procedure helps to define the existing strengths and areas for continued improvement for the supervisor. We'll discuss how to use the supervisor's information in Chapter 5.

When Will We Ever Learn?

Before we leave this chapter, we need to address one more extremely important issue: management/leadership training and development.

You know as well as I do some organizations have spent tens of thousands, even hundreds of thousands of dollars, on a training program (not including the cost of the employee's time) and ended up with a fine collection of manuals on employee bookshelves and little else. When will we ever learn that training per se does not change behavior? If you want to modify behavior, you must structure that change, measure it and hold people accountable for the change that does take place.

Another interesting aspect of most organizations that defies logic is working with employees to change their interpersonal behavior. What is done when an employee makes a technical mistake that reduces the quality of the product? The employee is corrected.

Now what happens when someone acts rudely, fails to communicate essential information or in some way acts outside of any of the statements listed in the examples of the TWMS? Most often, nothing constructive! Of course, there are plenty of famous expletives that are shouted during passionate moments of frustration, but that's about all. Do you find it interesting that we don't tolerate mistakes on the technical side of the business formula while at the same time we allow such mistakes on the people side?

We even have managers who, without question, talk disparagingly about their peers, treat their employees just as ugly and may be so brazen as to do the same with their supervisor. What is done about that? If anything, a note is written as a reminder to discuss this behavior during their next performance review, perhaps six months in the future.

As you can see, the TWMS serves as the anchor point to identify the common set of skills desired by all in the organization. Thus, the TWMS serves as a training vehicle to guide skill development.

We will revisit this issue later when we discuss coaching in the natural environment; the work place is the classroom for learning. At this point, I simply wanted to insert another extremely important characteristic of the TWMS.

In Summary

To successfully implement change we must know where we are going. The TeamWork Mission Statement describes our desired change effort and provides a set of written instructions for the management staff to lead the change effort.

It's also imperative to know one's point of origin as defined by measuring the current set of management practices. This measurement provides the opportunity to quantify change.

Rating supervisors on the TWMS, provides the advantage of being able to assist managers to be effective role models. That is, managers have the excellent opportunity to demonstrate their own willingness to create a culture of continuous improvement by being willing to continually improve their leadership/management skills.

> *To get where you want to go, you've got to know where you are and where you want to be.*

✦5✦

The Student Becomes the Teacher

What You Will Learn

You will learn how to create the working environment described in the TWMS.

Is the Student Ready for the Teacher?

The organization now has one or two sets of data. The company has been rated in terms of the TWMS and, when practical, supervisors have also been rated on the same characteristics. The next step in the process is to define action steps for what the supervisor and staff can do to improve the working relationship and create the desired culture. It is time to help each other be more successful.

The Supervisor Becomes the Student

The supervisor now becomes the student. The general procedure is to ask direct reports to brainstorm suggestions for what supervisors can do to improve working relationships with them or to continue their development as a supervisor. As you might have assumed, this process is sometimes difficult because this is a new role for employees.

The fear of retribution sometimes fosters the employees' desire to remain silent, but we have to break through this *silence is golden* paradigm before improvement can take place. With encouragement, employees usually complete the brainstorming process.

After a list of suggestions is generated and a consensus is reached, the list is presented to the supervisor for discussion. Following this conversation, the supervisor is asked to make suggestions as to what the staff can do to improve the working relationship. All of these action steps are recorded and distributed to provide daily reminders to everyone regarding the ongoing process. Progress will be evaluated within four to six weeks.

Since this is a new process for those involved and there is often some reluctance to participate, the process of completing this procedure can be more important than the actual content of the suggestions. At least the process of thinking about what can be done to help each other be more successful has finally begun! The typical procedure is to start this process at the top and work down. The active participation of the CEO is a demonstration of their commitment to change, which sends a strong message throughout the organization.

The following is an example of action steps established at the CEO level.

TeamWork Improvement Steps

Staff Recommends
1. Specific, agenda-driven meetings with explicit starting times.

2. A functional organizational chart, defined, then supported.

3. More clearly defined responsibilities and authority.

4. More immediate and frequent performance feedback.

5. New product/service ideas discussed before announcing them.

CEO Recommends

1. Give feedback instead of silently disagreeing with me.

2. Comply with defined time frames or immediately tell me it is not practical, instead of telling me a week or two later.

3. Support our decisions and present a common front.

4. Present facts to support your ideas.

Since these steps serve as a guide to day-to-day behavior, this agreement can serve as the conduit to remind each other when we are operating outside of the agreement.

For example, in this particular case, the direct reports asked their supervisor to more clearly define authority when delegating an assignment. Whenever any of this CEO's direct reports are not clear about their level of authority, they should only have to say, "I do not have a clear understanding about the level of my authority on this project, per our agreement."

The supervisor should do the same. For example, if the CEO notices that one of her staff is not supporting a decision, she need only say, "Remember our agreement to support decisions."

As you can imagine, this process tests the maturity level of the participants. Some managers resist the idea of encouraging their staff to be their teacher. And, as simple as the improvement suggestions might be, this could be the first time the supervisor and staff have openly discussed how they can improve their working relationship. Common sense tells us that we should do whatever we possibly can to help each other be more successful. How are we going to know what we need to do to help each other, if we don't talk about it?

We won't, which I would dare to say is the rule rather than the exception in most organizations. Remember, frustration is your organization's best friend. In this instance, we are using it to guide personal development.

The importance of completing this process is three-fold:

1. To create the mind-set of continuous improvement, it is important that each supervisor establishes the proper working environment. Everyone must feel free to suggest improvements in the working relationship.

2. Suggesting improvements in working relationships is often a sacred cow in the organization. Making such suggestions sends a clear message throughout the organization: We are serious about changing the corporate culture to support quality improvement.

3. The manager needs to lead the change process and act as a role model for others to follow.

Implementation

All parties receive a copy of the behavioral agreement which also serves as a report card, as illustrated in the following example. For variety, let's use a different set of action steps between a CEO and the staff in the following example.

❖ ❖ ❖

TeamWork Report Card

Instructions

Listed below are the agreed upon quality improvement steps to be completed by both the supervisor and the direct reports. Please use this Report Card as a daily reminder of how to help each other be more successful. Evaluate each other and yourself by simply marking the performance level achieved and bring this report with you to our next meeting.

	Improvement				
Staff Recommends	**Definite**	**Some**	**None**	**Worse**	**N/A**
1. Better understanding of objectives and expectations.	____	____	____	____	____
2. Let us present the facts before a decision is made.	____	____	____	____	____
3. Give us the opportunity to succeed by delegating authority to try our ideas.	____	____	____	____	____
4. Better scheduling of priorities to fit existing time frames.	____	____	____	____	____
CEO Recommends					
1. Be more assertive and present your recommendations.	____	____	____	____	____

❖ ❖ ❖

The supervisor is encouraged to discuss these action steps with employees during informal conversations and formally at a departmental meeting to demonstrate to the employees the seriousness of change.

Accountability Underwrites Change

In the case of the CEO, there is often not an "up-line" supervisor to receive a copy of the improvement action steps, thus placing additional pressures on the CEO to walk the talk of change.

At other management levels, the up-line supervisor receives a copy of the improvement action steps and discusses these action steps with each down-line supervisor. This procedure is important so up-line supervisors can assist their supervisors in the process of changing, plus up-line supervisors need to hold their supervisors accountable for the change. This procedure also sends the message from the top down that we are serious about implementing changes.

TeamWork is Quantified

Progress is measured with a four- to six-week time frame. Obviously, it is important to collect this data to provide each other with feedback.

Employees are asked to check the intensity measures to evaluate the progress made by both the supervisor and themselves. Progress, or the lack thereof, is discussed and the staff is asked to provide additional ideas on what the supervisor can do to improve.

The supervisor then joins the process and employees' feedback is presented and discussed. The supervisor is asked to provide his or her self-evaluation. Additional strategies are defined to be implemented for continued improvement as indicated by the evaluations.

The supervisor also presents ratings of the staff which are compared with the staff's self-evaluation. Again, if the ratings indicate a need for continued improvement, the strategies to be implemented are so defined.

Two progress reports are presented as examples. The first one does not include self-evaluations in an attempt to facilitate understanding of this process. The second one does include self-evaluations.

All parties receive a copy of the evaluations with a reminder to continue using the improvement steps as guidelines for day-to-day behavior.

The following Report Card may look more complicated than it actually is. I've explained each component in the statements immediately following the Report Card.

TeamWork Report Card

		Improvement				
	Definite	Some	None	Worse	N/A	Score
Staff Recommends	+2	+1	-1	-2		
1. Better understanding of objectives and expectations.	5	2	2	1		.80
2. Let us present the facts before a decision is made.	5	2	2	2		.70
3. Give us the opportunity to succeed by delegating authority to try our ideas.		6	4			.20
4. Better scheduling of priorities to fit existing time frames.	1	5	2	2		.10
		Improvement Index				**.45**

CEO Recommends	Definite +2	Some +1	None -1	Worse -2	N/A	Score
1. Be more assertive and present your recommendations.		1				1.00
Improvement Index						**1.00**

❖ ❖ ❖

As promised, the explanation of these numbers is presented in the following statements.

1. The numbers associated with each improvement intensity category represent the number of staff who rated the supervisor accordingly. For example, five rated the supervisor as making definite improvement explaining his objectives, two rated some improvement, two rated no improvement and one rated it worse.

2. Note that each improvement level has a numerical value, +2, +1, −1, and a −2.

3. Each mean is calculated by multiplying the frequency associated with the improvement category by its numerical value, e.g., five times a +2, two times a +1, two times a −1 and one times a −1. This sum is calculated and divided by the number of staff who rated the supervisor on that particular improvement step which is 10 in this case.

4. Any mean that exceeds zero represents improvement, while any mean equal to or less than zero indicates no improvement has been made.

5. The Improvement Index for the staff's recommendation is the mean of the means or scores associated with each of the four improvement steps.

6. The supervisor had one suggestion for improvement and rated the staff as making some improvement. Since he was the only one doing the rating, a score is used which is 1.00 in this case.

7. The Improvement Index is again the mean of the means associated with each improvement step, but since there was only one improvement step in this instance, the Improvement Index is also 1.00. Again, refer to the third statement for an interpretation of the Improvement Index.

This same procedure is consistently used for every Report Card. The individual means and Improvement Indexes are used to quantify TeamWork. Thus you can actually measure the progress of implementing the defined improvement steps and creating the culture described in the TWMS. These measurements also provide the opportunity to monitor progress over time.

The means show that this CEO made the most progress defining his expectations (mean = .80) and the least progress scheduling activities to fit existing time frames (mean = .10). Furthermore, he did not make much progress giving his staff the opportunity to succeed by delegating authority to try their ideas (mean = .20).

Actually the Improvement Index (mean = .45) suggests some progress was made overall although there is room for continued improvement.

The CEO rated the staff as making some improvement (score = 1.00) on being more assertive when presenting their recommendations.

Accountability is designed into these procedures by providing up-line supervisors a copy of the Report Card to discuss with their respective supervisors. In the particular example we're using with a CEO, we did not have his supervisors, the Board of Directors, involved in the process which placed additional pressure on the CEO to hold this process accountable.

Let's review one more example. Please note that this example presents self-evaluations as well as each party's evaluation of the other. The bold faced **X**s and **numbers** to the right of the slash marks represent self-evaluations.

❖ ❖ ❖

TeamWork Report Card

	Improvement					
Staff Recommends	**Definite**	**Some**	**None**	**Worse**	**N/A**	**Score**
	+2	+1	-1	-2		
1. Be more visible in the work environment.		4	3/**X**			.14
2. Talk to front-line employees.	1	4/**X**	2			.57
3. Learn more about employee job re-sponsibilities		3	3	/**X**	1	0.00
4. Be more relaxed.	1	**5/X**	1			.86
5. Listen to all the facts before mak-ing a decision.	3	3/**X**	1			1.14
6. Openly admit mis-takes.	1	**5/X**	1			.86
	Improvement Index					**.60**
Supervisor Recommends						**Score**
1. Accept construc-tive advice, improve perform-ance.	/1	**X**/2	/3		/1	1.00

	Definite	Some	None	Worse	N/A	Score
	+2	+1	-1	-2		
2. Be more creative and constantly look to improve the work environment.		X/5	/2			1.00
3. Share ideas with other managers.	/1	X/5			/1	1.00
4. Be more flexible for unforeseen circumstances and maintain responsibilities.	/1	X/3		/3		1.00
		Improvement Index				**1.00**

❖ ❖ ❖

Reviewing the means associated with each improvement step recommended by the staff shows that this supervisor made the most improvement and did really well listening to the facts before making a decision (mean = 1.14.) The least improvement was made in learning more about employee job responsibilities (mean = 0.00) and being more visible in the work environment (mean = .14).

The supervisor's self-evaluation (represented by the boldface "X") closely reflects that of the employees except he rated himself considerably lower in learning more about employee job responsibilities.

In this particular instance, the lack of measured progress served as a stimulus for action to make additional progress on achieving the suggested improvement steps.

As you can see, the supervisor rated the staff as making some improvement on each of the four improvement steps. Because he was the only one rating the staff, each score was 1.00. Consequently, the Improvement Index mean was also 1.00.

The staff's self-evaluation closely mirrored the supervisor's rating. Also note that some staff rated some of the improvement steps as non-applicable (NA) as there was not an opportunity to practice that particular improvement step.

Evaluating the Supervisor in Terms of the TWMS

Most organizations eventually reach the maturity level required to rate supervisors. When this occurs, information is obtained that is extremely beneficial for the supervisor and the employees.

The following example, involving a CEO, illustrates how the process works. The means are presented to identify the areas of strength and those needing improvement. Then a specific action plan is initiated.

TeamWork Mission Statement

In order to have a responsible working environment and promote cooperation, the company will empower its workforce through trust, delegation, communication and consistency.

	Strongly Disagree −3	Strongly Agree +3
		Mean

Responsible

1.	The work environment is safe.	2.67
2.	Productivity is achieved.	−.67
3.	Mistakes are readily admitted.	2.00
4.	Continuous self-improvement is encouraged.	2.50

Cooperation

5. Understand each other's needs. — 0.00
6. Willingly help each other. — 1.50
7. Listen to other people's opinions. — 1.25
8. Keep an open mind to accept other people's opinions. — 1.25
9. Willing to change to promote the organization. — 1.75

Trust

10. Confidential information is kept confidential. — .75
11. We do what we say we will do. — .25
12. We are kept informed. — −.25
13. Authority is delegated to us to do our job. — 2.00
14. Supervisors allow us to do our job. — 2.50
15. We are held accountable. — 2.25

Communication

16. We are free to express our ideas. — 2.00
17. We are encouraged to express our ideas. — 2.00
18. We receive timely feedback when a job is well done. — −.25
19. We receive constructive feedback as needed to improve job performance. — 0.00
20. Information is communicated accurately. — .50
21. Information is communicated timely. — −.50

Consistency

22. Policies and procedures are
applied consistently.   .25
23. Employees are treated fairly.   .50

As you can see, the means range from a −.67 to a +2.67. In order to develop the TeamWork Improvement Steps, we operationally defined the highest and lowest means to be the strengths and opportunities for improvement, respectively. In view of the fact that several value statements had the same mean, the decision was made to work with the 4 highest and lowest means as listed below with their associated means in parenthesis.

Strengths

1. Work environment is safe (2.67).
14. Supervisor allows us to do our job (2.50).
4. Continuous self-improvement is encouraged (2.50).
15. We are held accountable (2.25).

Opportunities for Improvement

2. Productivity is achieved (−.67)
21. Information is communicated timely (−.50)
12. We are kept informed (−.25).
18. We receive timely feedback when a job is
well done (−.25).

The process to development improvement steps is the same as previously described. A facilitator worked with the staff and generated the improvement steps which were presented to the CEO when he joined the meeting. The CEO, in turn, suggested improvement steps for the staff. These are listed below. Also note the staff elected to combine the communication issues of being kept informed, providing timely feedback for a job well done and communicating information in a timely manner into one category.

TeamWork Improvement Steps

Staff Recommends

Achieve Productivity

1. More rigid time frames associated with defined tasks.

2. Develop a "Priority List." Remain focused on these priority items.

Timely Feedback/Communication Issues

1. Continue the weekly staff meetings.

2. Keep us informed as you receive updated information.

3. Let us know your schedule, such as when you are out of town or out of the office for several hours.

4. More lead time on called meetings and distribute information through an agenda when possible.

5. More immediate performance feedback, both positive and constructive.

CEO Recommends

1. Remind me when I'm not doing what you have recommended.

2. Remind me when you are going to be out of the office.

Using the supervisor's ratings provides excellent feedback to that supervisor and allows the process to pinpoint specific areas for improvement.

Let's review another CEO as an example to illustrate this process.

TeamWork Mission Statement

To provide excellence in financial leadership, we work in harmony through open communications, respect and trust.

	Strongly Disagree −3	Strongly Agree +3 Mean

Harmony

1.	We understand each other's job responsibilities.	1.50
2.	We willingly help each other.	1.25
3.	We know what needs to be done and do it.	.75

Open Communications

4.	We are kept informed.	.50
5.	We are encouraged to express our ideas.	1.50
6.	We receive honest feedback.	2.25
7.	Managers listen to employees before decisions are made.	.25

Respect

8.	We care about each other.	1.75
9.	We are friendly to each other.	1.75
10.	We use each other's knowledge.	1.50

Trust

11.	We do what we say we will do.	.75
12.	We keep confidential information confidential.	2.50

13.   Managers delegate and let us
       do our job.   1.75

Grand Mean   **1.37**

The strengths were operationally defined to be the 5 highest means with the 5 lowest means representing areas for continuing improvement. These are listed below with their means in parenthesis.

Areas of Strength

12.   We keep confidential information confidential (mean = 2.50).

6.   We receive honest feedback (mean = 2.25).

8.   We care about each other (mean = 1.75).

9.   We are friendly to each other (mean = 1.75).

13.   Managers delegate and let us do our job (mean = 1.75).

Opportunities for Improvement

7.   Managers listen to employees before decisions are made (mean = .25).

4.   We are kept informed (mean = .50).

11.   We do what we say we will do (mean = .75).

3.   We know what needs to be done and do it (mean = .75).

2.   We willingly help each other (mean = 1.25).

Note the staff combined the third and fourth areas in the following TeamWork Improvement Steps based on their similarity.

TeamWork Improvement Steps

Staff Recommends

Listen before decisions are made.

1. Listen to our facts.

Be kept informed.

1. Provide staff the broad view of company's directions.
2. Consider once-per-month managers meeting.

We do what we say we will do, know what needs to be done and do it.

1. Hold the structure/individuals accountable for implementing what has been agreed to do.
2. Follow up with what he/she says needs to be done.

Willingly help each other.

1. Continue encouraging us to meet with the appropriate person/department to work on the issue.
2. Help us understand our responsibilities for common goals and hold us accountable for completing our responsibilities.

CEO Recommends

1. Decide if the matter really needs my attention or can somebody else deal with it.
2. Make suggestions as to what I can delegate to you.
3. Provide a written summary in advance of what we are going to discuss at scheduled meetings.

The advantage of using the supervisor rating by the staff is again obvious. Any supervisor who is clearly interested in continuous improvement will use this information for his personal growth and be the role model to create a work environment characterized by the TWMS in their department.

Ugly Ducklings Among the Swans

As you might imagine, the process is not always as smooth as I just described. There are managers who resist change. In one instance, the manager agreed to participate in the process, but almost as soon as I walked out of the building, he called a staff meeting and proceeded to announce, "This Larry Cole stuff is for the birds and it will be business as usual." To make matters worse, this was a senior level manager communicating this message to his down-line supervisors.

This gave me an opportunity to meet with this manager and the CEO to work out the details for cooperation with the process which the senior manager agreed to do. We also defined a procedure and schedule whereby the CEO would meet with the manager to ensure cooperation with the process.

Now here is the rest of the story: the CEO failed to cooperate with the procedure and schedule, so the process fell apart. The CEO, therefore, communicated the same message as the senior manager. After that, the CEO and I came to the agreement that the organization was interested in talking about change, but not really interested in changing.

As mentioned, this process tests the maturity level of the management structure. Over the years we have had managers opt to leave the organization rather than participate in the process. Other managers, like the preceding senior manager, decide not to walk the talk of the change process. When that happens, the organization only has two options. After everything possible has been done to encourage the individual to change, the organization then needs to decide how much resistance to change is acceptable without it being a major deterrent to the change process.

During this consideration, managers may be reassigned, or the process continues to be implemented while recognizing the resistance of this particular manager. The last option is to help those who resist a career change.

This resistance to change defies logic, doesn't it? All that is being done is to identify what can be done to improve the working relationships. Common sense tells us that it is not only appropriate, but right. Even those who resist change will agree with this truism. They will even make such statements as, "we need to do everything we can to promote excellent working relationships and improve morale, which will improve productivity and quality." But what they are really saying is "*you* change; leave me alone." Without belaboring the point, we must remember the fact that *change begins with me*.

In Summary

The process for continued improvement simply requires that both parties be willing to:

- Identify action steps to improve the working relationship
- Implement the action steps
- Evaluate progress

Everyone is our teacher if we have the good sense

to be open to learning.

❖6❖

Building Stronger Bridges

What You Will Learn

You will learn about an easily implemented procedure to meet the needs of your other internal customers: other departments which need your assistance.

Common Sense Partnerships

Doesn't it make sense that we would do whatever needs to be done to help our peer departments be successful? If we knew one of our internal customers needed us to do something, we would complete this responsibility with the highest quality and on time, right? If we knew that our peer department depended upon us every day, all day long to complete our responsibilities with the highest quality, we would break our necks to make certain those needs were met, right?

And if we knew something was wrong that adversely affected our internal customers, we would communicate what is wrong immediately and effectively. Correct? Common sense and common courtesy would dictate that we would do all of the above, even if we haven't breathed the words "continuous improvement" or the "TeamWork Mission Statement," right? WRONG!

Something happens to us when we walk through the doors into our place of employment. We seem to lose our common sense, courtesy and respect for our responsibilities. We just go a little crazy! Walls go up and territorialism reigns. We stop speaking to each other. Or when we do talk, we make certain we only tell half-truths, give partial information, or create a mixed word salad so as to confuse everyone.

If ugly words weren't bad enough, we might add anger, spitting, cussing, cold stares, the silent treatment and a red face to make our point. Now, we're communicating! Our department is going to win at all costs. After all if it wasn't for us there would not be a company in the first place!

What's really crazy about this mess is that every department needs every other department in order for the organization to achieve a high level of success. As a matter of fact, the individuals within the organization need each other to be successful. Can the CEO run the organization by him or herself? Can the production department run the organization by itself? What about sales? Or the accounting department? Can any one supervisor run the whole department single-handedly? The answer to all of these question is not only "no," but *"heck no!"*

But you certainly wouldn't be able to tell that by some of our words and actions, would you? You would think that the management structure would at least realize the importance of the interdepartmental working relationships, wouldn't you? After all, these managers are supposed to be some of the brightest and best people in the organization, right? What happens to all this intelligence?

Have you ever wondered why we go a little crazy and tell other departments, through our words and actions, that we're important and we're not going to listen to them? We do our thing as if we were an island. But when asked by an outsider, "Are you cooperating to produce a quality product or service?" lies jump out of our mouths faster than we can blink an eye.

There are numerous sources that contribute to such territorialism. Some of them follow below. I'm sure you can add others to this list.

- Lack of common goals
- Different departmental values
- Stupidity
- Personality issues . . . I don't like you
- Power plays and one-upmanship
- Insecurity and ego games
- Lack of understanding of what one department needs from another

Customer Service Wheel

The process of common sense partnerships begins with a customer service wheel to define internal customers. That is, a given department is placed in the middle as the hub of the service wheel. The spokes represent internal customers. Operationally defined, internal customers are those departments that depend upon the given department for a product or service, or that a given department receives a product or service from. Thus, that department is either giving to or receiving from the internal customers.

Figure Four presents a service wheel for the human resource office. Every office interacts with human resource; thus, every department is its customer.

A second example is illustrated in Figure Five.

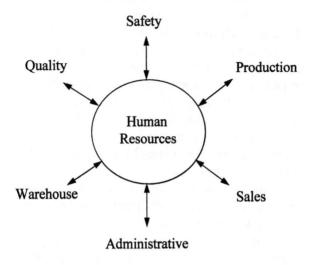

Figure 4

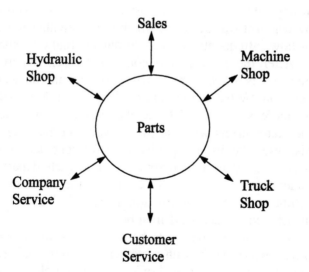

Figure 5

Once internal customers are identified, each department is asked to prioritize up to three departments with whom it needs to improve its working relationship. This improvement can be in terms of product/service, meeting defined specifications, accuracy, or timeliness, as well as the more traditional interpersonal relationships of cooperating in a friendly manner and receiving complete information in a timely and accurate fashion. It matters not what the subject matter is. If it is a source of frustration then it serves as a signal for improvement. It's your organization's best friend.

Following this prioritization, a matrix is completed to more easily identify which department has been selected by any given department.

An attempt is made to give each department its number one selection. However, it's possible that a given department could be selected as number one by several departments and it becomes a bit difficult for a given department to focus on more than two other departments at any given time. Frequently a department is surprised by whom it was selected, which is just another indicator of how infrequently we talk to our internal customers.

After the pairings are completed, each department manager is asked to meet with the staff and answer the question, "What can the paired department do to help us be more successful?" Once the lists are completed, a facilitator meets with the two department managers and discusses the list of quality improvement action steps presented by each department. After each department understands and agrees to complete the recommended action steps, this information is recorded and a copy distributed to each staff member.

The example below is between a customer service office (which works with customers within the office) and the customer service field office (whose employees work with customers outside of the office). The following illustration includes the typical instructions and format for evaluation.

TeamWork Report Card

Instructions

These are the action steps to help each other be more successful. Please review these daily and in a few weeks you will evaluate each other and yourselves by simply checking a progress category for each statement.

	Improvement				
Field Office Needs	**Definite**	**Some**	**None**	**Worse**	**N/A**
1. All customer account information entered in computer by end of day.	____	____	____	____	____
2. All paid collections to field reps by 9 a.m.	____	____	____	____	____
3. Notify field reps of partial-paid accts. made in office and void shutoff notice.	____	____	____	____	____
4. Provide realistic time frames for field reps to respond to customer requests.	____	____	____	____	____
Office Personnel Needs					
1. Field reps to be more courteous to customers.	____	____	____	____	____

	Definite	Some	None	Worse	N/A
2. Provide specific information on service orders.	___	___	___	___	___
3. Make customer contact before preparing work orders.	___	___	___	___	___
4. Send work orders to proper dispatcher.	___	___	___	___	___

❖ ❖ ❖

Employees receive a copy of this behavioral agreement to serve as a daily reminder for what each department has agreed to do to assist the paired department to be more successful.

A copy of these action steps is provided to the up-line supervisors, who then discusses them with their respective down-line supervisors for accountability purposes.

After four to six weeks, these action steps are evaluated. This evaluation can occur between managers, or each manager can ask the staff to evaluate the paired department success at completing the recommended action steps by simply marking the intensity scale on the Report Card. Incorporating employees into the evaluation process is desired of course, but sometimes the situation prevents that from happening. Each department also rates itself in terms of meeting expectations recommended by the paired department.

The first example is one in which only the managers completed the evaluations (self-evaluations are included in bold print after the slash [/] mark). We used one from the financial services industry to demonstrate flexibility of this process across industries.

❖ ❖ ❖

TeamWork Report Card
Tellers and Proof Departments

	Improvement					
Tellers Need From Proof	Definite	Some	None	Worse	N/A	Score
	+2	+1	-1	-2		
1. Proof needs VISA information before meeting with the tellers.		X/X				1.00
2. Proof to pick up all work from the bin daily.		X/X				1.00
		Improvement Index				**1.00**
Proof Needs From Tellers						
1. Correctly enter check amounts.	/X		X			−1.00
2. Make general ledger tickets.		X/X				1.00
3. Tear tabs off end of tickets, deposit slips and carbon.	/X		X			−1.00
4. Check endorsement on ABC company.		X/X				1.00
5. Make sure ribbons print on tickets.		X/X				1.00
		Improvement Index				**.20**

❖ ❖ ❖

Interpretation is identical to that described in the previous chapter. Because one person rated each department, each improvement step has a score rather than a mean and the improvement index is a mean of these scores. Any score or mean greater than zero indicates progress. Conversely a score or mean of zero or less suggests a lack of progress.

The data shows the proof department made progress in meeting the needs of the tellers. Overall, the tellers made progress helping the proof department with the exceptions of correctly entering check amounts and tearing tabs off the end of tickets, deposit slips and carbon. The self-evaluations show the tellers thought they had made some progress in these areas as well. The differences in perception provided an opportunity for continued improvement for the tellers to meet the proof department's needs.

The following example included the employees ratings.

❖ ❖ ❖

TeamWork Report Card
Parts and Service

| | *Improvement* | | | | | |
Service Needs From Parts	Definite	Some	None	Worse	N/A	Mean
	+2	+1	-1	-2		
1. Respond to parts quotes more quickly.		/3	2/1	10		−1.83
2. Fill parts orders more quickly.		/4	2	10		−1.83
3. Let us know when there is a problem locating a part.	/2	2/2	2	8		−1.33

	Definite	Some	None	Worse	N/A	Mean
	+2	+1	-1	-2		
4. Keep us informed about the status of back orders.		/4	3	9		−1.75
	Improvement Index					**−1.68**
Parts Needs From Service						
1. Complete information on parts orders.		2/12	2	2		0.00
2. Accurate information on parts orders.		2/12	2			0.00
	Improvement Index					**0.00**

❖ ❖ ❖

The means show that the parts department did not make progress in meeting the needs of the service department. Several staff even rated the parts department's performance as being worse. The service department did not make progress either.

Even though two staff members from the parts department thought the service department had some improvement, two did not so the overall mean for each of these improvement steps was zero measuring no improvement.

Here is an excellent opportunity to recall that *frustration is the organization's best friend.* As of this writing, the respective managers report significant progress being made.

The service department, in this instance, was doing what so many departments do in other organizations. An internal customer is not meeting its needs, so what does it do about it? Outside of griping and complaining to each other, usually nothing. Isn't it ironic that we don't know the frustrations of our internal customers unless they tell us? I'm sure you recognized the bit of tongue in cheek humor in that statement. But what is even more ironic is that we most often don't even ask our internal customers what we are doing to create inconveniences and frustrations in their lives.

We just ass-u-me, "if one of our internal customers has a problem with us they will surely tell us." And, of course, that department has made the assumption that "talking to them won't do any good anyway" so the frustrations are not turned into opportunities for growth. Instead, frustration just continues to be destructive energy instead of serving as fuel for improvement.

In Summary

The system remains the same for both intra- and interdepartment improvement: define improvement steps that can assist someone be more successful, implement these steps and evaluate progress. The extent the department manager implements the actions steps is the extent that manager leads by example to communicate the seriousness of continuous improvement. There is no other way! Change occurs from the top down at every level in the organization.

Using this simple system over and over again to implement the desired corporate culture creates a corporate mind-set of continuous improvement.

Helping those who depend upon us to be more successful is being more successful.

❖7❖

Revisiting the TeamWork Mission Statement

What You Will Learn

It is time for the employees to rate the organization on the TWMS and compare these numbers with the benchmark data.

The Proof of the Pudding Is in the Numbers

As we mentioned before, accountability is the name of the game. To make people accountable, the change taking place must be measured.

You measure change when you alter a personal habit, so why not do the same thing in an organization? For example, there are several indicators for change when starting an exercise program. First is the actual participation in the exercise, let's say four times a week. That's a measured change from being a couch potato. Second is the level of activity. Jogging around the block may be difficult when you first start exercising. Later you'll use time or the number of miles as the system to measure progress.

Writing this book represents a major change for me. To begin with, I questioned the availability of time. But then I began looking and found about five hours a week I could devote to writing. Other measures of progress included the number of chapters completed and then the revisions, revisions and more revisions.

The Improvement Indexes used in Chapters Five and Six were used to measure change.

Now it is time to measure change again. At the beginning of the process, employees were asked to evaluate the organization in terms of the TWMS. After several months of addressing these issues, employees are once again asked to participate in rating the company on the value statements contained in the TeamWork Mission Statement document.

For illustrative purposes, three examples measuring organizational progress are included. Two of these will show measured improvement while the third does not.

Progress

The following data shows the progress that can be made when an organization is committed to implement the corporate culture described in their TeamWork Mission Statement.

TeamWork Mission Statement

Maximizing employee involvement to create a harmonious environment that encourages mutual trust and self-esteem through communication and cooperation.

	Strongly Disagree −3 1st Mean	Strongly Agree +3 2nd Mean

Maximizing Employee Involvement

1. We receive needed training for the job. .58 .90
2. We have resources needed to do the job. .94 1.11

Harmonious Environment

3. Common goals are clearly defined. 1.33 1.61
4. All departments are working to achieve these common goals. .76 1.03
5. All departments are treated fairly. −.29 .87
6. We are friendly to each other. 1.85 2.16
7. We enjoy our work. 1.59 2.00
8. We are honest with each other. 1.06 1.58
9. We can depend upon each other to do what has been agreed to. 1.17 1.62
10. We keep confidential information confidential. 1.29 1.75
11. My supervisor/manager lets me do my job. 1.70 2.26
12. We practice delegating down to the lowest level. .86 1.44

Self-Esteem

13. We are trained to do the job right. 1.00 1.36
14. We are quick to praise a job well done. .22 .84

15.	Mistakes are viewed as opportunities to learn.	.59	1.24
16.	Discipline is completed in a private setting.	.96	1.70
17.	My supervisor remains calm when a mistake has been made.	.97	1.76
18.	My supervisor respects my specific knowledge.	1.23	1.84
19.	My supervisor supports my decisions.	1.24	1.84

Communication

20.	We are encouraged to provide input into decision making.	.87	1.40
21.	My supervisor listens to understand my point of view.	1.10	1.62
22.	We have a win/win environment when discussing different viewpoints.	.78	1.44
23.	Feedback is received in a timely manner.	.52	1.08

Cooperation

24.	Departments understand each other's priorities.	.33	.81
25.	Departments are working together for the good of each department.	.44	.99
26.	We are willing to help each other.	1.20	1.72
27.	We are cross-trained to help each other.	.19	.86
	Grand Mean	**.91**	**1.44**

Operationally, we defined significant improvement to be an increase in the means of at least .50. The five lowest means represent areas for continued improvement, while strengths were operationally defined to be the five highest means.

Since 16 of the 27 statements had a difference score that exceeded .50, this organization made great progress.

The five significant strength areas are:

11. The supervisors allow employees to do their job (2.26).

6. We are friendly to each other (2.16).

7. We enjoy their work (2.00).

18. My supervisor respects my specific knowledge (1.84).

19. My supervisor supports my decisions (1.84).

The five growth opportunities are:

24. Departments understand each other's priorities (.81).

14. We are quick to praise a job well done (.84).

27. We are cross-trained to help each other (.86).

5. All departments are treated fairly (.87).

25. Departments working together for the good of each department (.99).

An examination of these areas for improvement shows some similarity between them. They can be categorized in the following general areas: training, providing pats-on-the back and interdepartment issues. Each was identified as an area for continued focus in this organization.

Using The TeamWork Mission Statement Data

This data guides the organization's efforts to develop additional strategies for implementing the TeamWork Mission Statement. That is, the organization can identify and implement strategies for improving training, providing positive feedback for a job well done and continue to improve interdepartment coordination.

In this instance, some of the strategies could be as follows.

Training

- Involve employees to identify training needed to do their job. The employees in this organization wanted more training on how to service some very technical equipment. Some managers in this organization have discussed establishing a minimum number of hours for continued education per year.

- Design and implement the training process.

- The issues associated with cross-training were defined to be within a particular department since each department specializes in such technical equipment that it would not be feasible to cross-train all employees for each department.

Treat Departments Fairly

- Through discussion with employees, identify which departments are not treated fairly and provide examples of such treatment.

- Once identified, the organization can implement a procedure to ensure equal treatment.

Interdepartment Issues

- Continue to focus on the interdepartment process to identify the needs of internal customers, implement action steps to meet these needs and evaluate progress.

Success stories are always encouraging. Let's examine one more for illustration purposes.

TeamWork Mission Statement

Realizing each individual is a vital link in our organization, we will communicate honestly, exhibit respect, trust, and loyalty, acknowledge a job well done and cooperate toward our common goals.

	Strongly Disagree −3 1st Mean	Strongly Agree +3 2nd Mean

Individual Is a Vital Link

1. Realize individual contribution is important. — .91 — 1.32
2. Policies are consistently applied to all employees. — .12 — .96

Honest Communication

3. We are kept informed. — −.24 — .88
4. We are encouraged to express our ideas. — .11 — 1.10
5. We listen to each other without interrupting. — .30 — 1.35
6. Our opinions are used. — −.26 — .87
7. We are open-minded to logical change. — .40 — 1.29

Respect

8. We are treated as the company's most important asset. — −.45 — .36
9. We care for each other as persons. — .57 — 1.11

10.	We are treated fairly.	−.31	.59

Trust

11.	Supervisors allow us to do our work.	1.13	1.69
12.	We do what we agree to do.	1.42	1.68
13.	Confidential information is kept confidential.	1.20	1.71

Loyalty

14.	We speak highly of the company.	.69	1.24
15.	We speak highly of each other.	.72	1.00

Acknowledging a Job Well Done

16.	Positive recognition is received.	.17	1.00
17.	All departments are considered equal.	−.70	1.14

Cooperating

18.	We understand other department's needs.	−.22	.78
19.	We are willing to help each other.	.88	1.31
20.	We treat each other like customers.	.05	.90

Common Goal

21.	The company's common goals are defined.	.70	1.41
22.	These goals are communicated.	.27	1.20
23.	We work together to achieve the common goals.	.39	1.08
	Grand Mean	**.25**	**1.32**

Using the same operational definitions as previously mentioned, 19 of 23 statements showed improvement exceeding .50. Again, the five highest and lowest means represent the strengths and areas for improvement, respectively.

The following were defined as relative strengths as they represent the highest 5 means:

13. Confidential information is kept confidential (1.71).

11. Supervisors allow us to do our work (1.69).

12. We do what we agree to do (1.68).

21. The company's common goals are defined (1.41).

5. We listen to each other without interrupting (1.35).

Areas for continued improvement or those with means less than 1.00 are:

8. We are treated as the company's most important asset (.36).

10. We are treated fairly (.59).

18. We understand other department's needs (.78).

6. Our opinions are used (.87).

3. We are kept informed (.88).

First, note that all of these means showed significant improvement. In some instances, they approached an improvement of 1.0. An examination of these show three clusters of behaviors. First is the way employees are treated, second is understanding each other's needs and the third is a communications issue.

From an overall standpoint, this organization could expect to make continued progress by developing strategies for these three areas. These strategies could include:

Employees Are Treated Fairly

- Identify, through discussion with staff, which policies are not applied consistently to all employees.

- Once identified, the organization can implement a procedure to ensure equal treatment of all employees.

Understanding Other Department's Needs

- Continue to focus on the interdepartment process that was previously discussed to identify the needs of internal customers, implement action steps to meet these needs and evaluate progress.

Communication Issues

- Structure employee input through staff meetings and project teams, and ask for employee recommendations upon bringing a problem to be solved to their supervisor.

- Keep employees informed through staff meetings and internal newsletters and bulletins. Also, ask staff to identify incidents of when they heard something or were not kept informed. Use each of these incidents as learning opportunities to implement a procedure to keep employees informed.

Obviously, employee input into defining strategies for continued improvement is crucial to success.

All Is Not Always Well

Now it's time to look at the other side of the coin. Our next example followed the process and the Improvement Indexes showed progress had been achieved both within and between departments. As you will see, however, there is very little change between the two measurements of the TWMS.

Before presenting the data, I might also point out that the validity of employee surveys depends upon the honesty of those completing the survey. In this instance, several employees told me after collecting the benchmark data that they knew many employees rated the organization high in fear of retribution. Thus, the benchmark numbers were artificially inflated by the fear factor. This fact was discussed with the staff prior to the second measurement and they were asked to be honest in their rating of both the organization and supervisor. While there is no way to deduct the artificial inflation of the benchmark data (for all intents and purposes the numbers show that this organization made very little headway), this company had progressed to the point that *supervisors* were also rated. That is measured progress, isn't it?

As you can tell, this example points out the naked truth that employee surveys can be manipulated by the fear factor or anything else that drives a lack of honesty. That's a problem, but it's something we have to live with. We must remember this margin of error.

TeamWork Mission Statement

To provide excellence in financial leadership we work in harmony through open communications, respect and trust.

	Strongly Disagree –3 1st Mean	Strongly Agree +3 2nd Mean

Harmony

1. We understand each other's job responsibilities. .79 .60

2.	We willingly help each other.	1.19	1.21
3.	We know what needs to be done and do it.	.95	1.23

Open Communications

4.	We are kept informed.	–.24	–.05
5.	We are encouraged to express our ideas.	–.04	.16
6.	We receive honest feedback.	.14	.14
7.	Managers listen to employees before decisions are made.	–.31	–.49

Respect

8.	We care about each other.	1.89	1.38
9.	We are friendly to each other.	1.81	1.33
10.	We use each other's knowledge.	1.25	.91

Trust

11.	We do what we say we will do.	1.56	.88
12.	We keep confidential information confidential.	1.89	1.34
13.	Managers delegate and let us do our jobs.	1.13	1.21
	Grand Mean	**.92**	**.76**

As you can see, there is very little movement in the means. Five of the means showed a slight increase while the remaining either stayed the same or showed a decrease.

The relative strengths for this organization are operationally defined to be those five characteristics with the higher means and these are:

8.   We care about each other (1.38).

12. We keep confidential information confidential (1.34).

9. We are friendly to each other (1.33).

3. We know what needs to be done and do it (1.23).

2. We willingly help each other (1.21).

13. Managers delegate and let us do our job (1.21).

The opportunities for growth are those five characteristics with the lowest means:

7. Managers listen to employees before making decisions (–.49).

4. We are kept informed (–.05).

6. We receive honest feedback (.14).

5. We are encouraged to express our ideas (.16).

1. We understand each other's job responsibilities (.60).

The lack of progress turned out to be a great stimulus for growth for this organization. The information got their attention. The CEO conducted a staff meeting to present the data and commented, "We can and we will do better!" The management staff agreed and this firm is walking the journey of progress.

In Summary

Now you've seen the results of the process beginning with the TeamWork Mission Statement, completing intra- and interdepartment TeamWork improvement steps and remeasuring the TeamWork Mission Statement. I would like to be so bold as to state, "I can guarantee the process will work. But I can't guarantee you will work the process."

*Receiving feedback is the only way
we know if anything has changed.*

❖**8**❖

Living the TeamWork Mission Statement

What You Will Learn

You will be shown several different procedures to make the TeamWork Mission Statement an integral component of your corporate culture.

What Happens Now?

That's the looming question most people ask after learning about the process described in the preceding chapters. It's not only a logical question, but also a very important one. Hopefully, you don't want all this work to become the next idea laid to rest in the idea of the month cemetery. Unfortunately, there's always enough room for one more idea to be buried in this bottomless pit.

Before proceeding, there's another issue that needs to be mentioned: organizations are very similar to the proverbial rose garden that grows weeds unless you implement a continuing process to remove them. Organizations are constantly growing weeds. We call such weeds vicious rumors, gossip and other ugly words. People are going to talk about something to fill the time vacuum that exists. If there is nothing good to talk about, people will generate other subject matter to discuss. Some of these won't contribute to the organization's good health.

The TeamWork Mission Statement provides you the tool to fill the vacuum with words and actions that promote positive changes.

Walking and Talking the TWMS

If the TWMS is going to work for you, the management structure must walk the walk and talk the talk— every day, all day long. This is a bit of an over dramatization of a fantasy world, because I've not seen many saints walking around disguised as managers. A manager's temper will be lost, ugly words will come out of his mouth, employees will not receive the "atta boy/girl" they thought was due and the manager will one day not cooperate with another department.

Whenever these things happen, the manager is managing by example. This gives permission to employees to act the same. I've never participated in writing a TWMS with such descriptive words. But just as sure as you are reading this book and machines are going to break, managers are going to be human and make errors.

We must, however, resist the temptation to use being a human as an excuse for our errors, because doing so can open the flood gates of behaviors that are not consistent with the desired culture. Then weeds grow in the garden.

Structure TeamWork for the Team to Work

The question remains, "How to make the TeamWork Mission Statement live?" The remainder of this chapter is devoted to answering this question. In doing so the following suggestions will be discussed in some detail.

TeamWork Mission Statement Lives

- Scheduling customer service meetings
- Walking the talk of the TWMS and being a role model
- Teaching in the natural environment
- Conducting annual evaluations of the TWMS, organization and supervisor

Scheduled Customer Service Meetings

The first procedure is to schedule departmental customer service meetings to evaluate progress of working with the internal customers we have been addressing.

In terms of intradepartmental TeamWork, the manager and staff can regularly evaluate progress of the Team-Work improvement strategies and define additional ones for continued improvement. It is imperative to create the mind-set to look at every interaction under a magnifying glass to identify other points of frustration or those specific behaviors that can be improved. The manager will have to lead this effort for this process to become an integral component of the corporate culture.

The same is true for interdepartment TeamWork improvements. At designated times, every department focuses on one of its internal customers, reviews progress of defined improvement steps and redefines additional improvements to be made. The up-line supervisors receive this information and continue to hold the down-line managers responsible for changes. This process can be completed monthly, bimonthly or quarterly and becomes an integral component of your culture—it's just the way you do things in your organization. This process occurs like clockwork to send the message that living and creating a corporate culture described by the TWMS is important in this organization.

You may question the logic of a monthly schedule to address the people side of your business, but old habits die hard and consistent attention has to be focused on the new behavior to successfully change.

I can hear the complaint that your organization is already "meetinged to death" and the customer service meeting notion just adds another nail to the coffin. I understand the dilemma, but most organizations have operations meetings to discuss production, service and administrative issues, right? So are you suggesting it's okay to schedule meetings to discuss the technical side of your business but not the people side? Surely not, since it is the people side of the business that determines the efficiency and success of the technical side.

All I am suggesting is that you give the people side of your business the same attention the operational side receives. You can fold the customer service agenda items into your operations meeting if you make certain these agenda items receive their due attention. You can ensure that by scheduling these items first. If not, there is the danger of them getting lost by taking a back seat to the operational issues.

Designating independent meetings for internal customer service sends a very strong message about the seriousness of these issues. That's the song you want sung throughout the organization isn't it?

To help you plan a monthly customer service agenda, let me offer the following content areas.

Customer Service Meeting Agenda

- Regularly scheduled reviews of intra- and inter-departmental TeamWork improvement strategies to walk the talk of the TWMS.

- Identify areas of confusion as to who has the responsibility and authority to make decisions regarding production and service issues, particularly if you want to empower employees to make decisions closer to your internal customer.

- Review the TeamWork Mission Statement evaluations.

- Review journal articles, books (like this one!) and videos.

- Ask other department representatives to explain the responsibilities of their department to foster understanding of internal customer's needs.

- Review the principles in conducting excellent meetings to minimize time lost through not starting on time, straying from agenda items, random conversations and discussing items to death without making decisions.

- Identify sources of frustration. As we've said, frustration is your organization's best friend if you use it to grow.

- Identify "boo-boos" which inconvenience other employees. Use the staff to define how to not only "fix" the issue, but to define what can be done to go the extra mile to offer value, define how the process can be changed to ensure the boo-boo doesn't occur again. Train staff accordingly.

- Use the Stop and Think training model which is discussed later in this chapter.

Walking the Talk as a Role Model

This is the second procedure for making certain the TWMS lives in your department and organization. Don't let me confuse you about the importance of serving as an effective role model by listing this second in the series. Actually, managers serve as a role model every day, all day long. Managers often forget that everything they do gives their staff permission to do the same. Although I've known managers, as you have, who operated with the management philosophy *"Do as I say and not as I do."* That doesn't fly in today's work environment.

It is imperative for the management structure to act out the value statements contained in their TWMS, to send the message "We are serious about creating this culture."

There are a couple of alternatives to structure this role modeling. The first is to use the value statements contained in the TWMS as guidelines for your behavior. To illustrate this process, let's use a TWMS we previously discussed.

To achieve our common goals, we are committed to TeamWork characterized by open communication, honesty, trust, respect and a positive mental attitude.

The value statements for this mission statement were defined as follows:

Common Goals
1. We exceed our customers' expectations to provide a quality product.

Committed
1. We are dedicated to the success of the company.

TeamWork
1. We understand each other's needs.
2. We willingly help each other succeed.
3. Problems are solved in a win/win manner.

Open Communication

1. We are encouraged to express our ideas.
2. We are kept informed.
3. We listen to facts before making a decision.

Honesty

1. We represent information accurately.
2. We look at situations objectively.

Trust

1. We do what we say we will do.
2. We work in a safe environment.
3. Managers support employees decisions.
4. Confidential information is kept confidential

Respect

1. All departments are considered equal.
2. We accept each other's ideas.

Positive Mental Attitude

1. We look for the good in everything.
2. We are friendly to each other.
3. We are courteous to each other.

Everyone needs to use these value statements as daily instructions to guide their behaviors.

Walking the talk of the TWMS needs to be a scheduled agenda item for the department's customer service meetings. The team needs to evaluate their success at creating this culture. The manager also needs direct feedback regarding his or her success at being an effective role model. At such feedback meetings, it is important to share success stories as well as examples of specific incidences when a member of the team did not live up to the defined expectations. Remember any variation from the expectations serve as points of frustration to identify areas for improvement. Let's use frustration as a friend.

Because such team/department meetings can be somewhat sensitive, the process can be made easier with specific times scheduled to review progress rather than leaving it open for a team member to indicate a need for a feedback meeting. Of course, flagrant violations of the TWMS need to be dealt with immediately through meetings with the individual(s) involved or via a team/department meeting.

A Better Way

There's no question that completing the above process can be extremely beneficial to ensure that everyone is together. The second alternative to walk the talk of a role model is to take the TWMS to another level of development. For example, as a manager how do you know when "customer expectations are being met?" or how to demonstrate "you are committed to the company's success?"

Wouldn't it be better to further define the value statements so everyone knows what can be done to walk the talk of each value statement? In other words, would additional instructions to guide behavior be beneficial? For example, as a manager or department, do you know when:

- Customer expectations are being met?
- You are committed to the company's success?

To illustrate this process, let's use the same TWMS and operationally define the value statements. Before doing that, though, let me minimize your concerns regarding the number of operational definitions listed for each of the value statements. I am listing several to stimulate ideas for you and your work environment, not to overwhelm you. You may limit the number of your definitions. It's better to provide a couple of operational definitions and do them well than do a miserable job trying to implement a large number. The point is to find something that works for you.

TeamWork Mission Statement
Walking the Talk

We Walk the Talk When We . . .

Common Goals
1. We exceed our customers' expectations to provide a quality product.

1. Know their expectations.
2. Exceed these expectations.
3. Do something special.

Commitment
1. We are dedicated to the success of the company.

1. Define individual, departmental and company goals.
2. Hold people accountable to achieve these goals.
3. Review progress regularly.
4. Implement change.
5. Evaluate the manager in terms of the TWMS.

TeamWork
1. We understand each other's needs.

1. Define what we need from each other to achieve departmental goals and hold each other accountable.

2. Establish both intra-
   and interdepartmental
   performance indi-
   cators.
3. Implement an evalu-
   ation procedure for
   internal customers to
   evaluate each other.

2. We willingly help
   each other succeed.

1. Do special things for
   each other.
2. Regularly monitor
   each other's perfor-
   mance.
3. Cooperatively
   respond to requests
   for assistance.
4. Make it easy for
   internal customers to
   provide us feedback.

3. Problems are solved
   in a win/win manner.

1. Define each other's
   needs.
2. Solidify your
   common goals.
3. Use scientific method
   of problem solving.
4. Let others know
   when using their
   ideas.
5. Tell "why" an idea is
   not used.

Open Communication

1. We are free to express our ideas.

   1. Ask for employee input.
   2. Use teams.

2. We are kept informed.

   1. Schedule open forums.
   2. Regularly schedule department meetings.
   3. Distribute minutes of meetings.
   4. Use bulletin/ newsletter.
   5. Present reports on performance goals, financial, customer service data and what's going on in the company.

3. We listen to facts before making a decision.

   1. Make data-based decisions using pro-duction and financial reports, and feedback on goals.
   2. Use the scientific method for problem solving.
   3. Ask for input/recom-mendations and tell how this input im-pacted the decision.

Honesty/ Communication

1. Tell them what is going on.

   1. Provide data: pro-duction/service

levels, financial information, audit results (safety, quality), customer satisfaction numbers, minutes, etc.
2. Share vision, goals, objectives and provide variance reports.
3. Dispel rumors by providing facts.

2. Information is represented accurately.

1. Same as above.

3. We look at situations objectively.

1. Use scientific method for solving problems.
2. Listen to and understand others' input.

Trust
1. We do what we say we will do.

1. Keep commitments, meet time lines.
2. Provide progress reports/feedback.

2. We work in a safe environment.

1. Document accident reports.
2. Conduct safety audits.
3. Do regularly scheduled safety training.

3. Management support of employees' decisions.

1. Provide supportive feedback.
2. Use mistakes as learning tools.
3. Give credit when credit is due.

4. Confidential information is kept confidential.

1. Honor confidentiality.
2. Report when can't provide all the information.
3. Make it easy to report when confidentiality has been violated.

Respect
1. All departments are considered equal.

1. Consistently apply policies and procedures.
2. Cooperate equally with all departments (meet their needs).

2. We accept each other's ideas.

1. Ask for others' ideas.
2. Use others' ideas.
3. Use teams.
4. Give credit when credit is due.
5. Catch someone doing something right.

Positive Mental Attitude
1. We look for the good in everything.

1. Exhibit a consistent positive mood.

2. Ask "What did you learn? How did you benefit?"
3. Ask, "What do you recommend to solve the problem?"
4. When we see/hear people talking about "I can't," ask them to think "I can."
5. Refrain from listening to rumors.
6. Discuss what's right instead of what's wrong.
7. Talk about opportunities instead of problems.

2. We are friendly to each other.

1. Greet each other.
2. Talk to each other about personal lives.
3. Consider other people's needs.
4. Look for the good/ accentuate the positive.

3. We are courteous to each other.

1. Be polite to colleagues.
2. Be considerate of others' needs and cooperate to meet them.
3. Recognize how others feel and ask, "Is there anything I

can do to help you
feel better?"
4. If you can't say
something positive,
refrain from saying
anything.

TWMS and Leadership Development

You are now using the TWMS as the anchor for your management and leadership development process. Expectations are clearly defined for managers to implement.

Skill development via classroom instruction will become an integral component of implementing the TWMS which speaks to another advantage of this process—the TWMS provides definite guidelines for academic preparation.

The skills necessary to implement the TWMS are crucial. The TWMS we have been working with suggests the following training areas.

- The role of a supervisor as a leader, role model, manager and teacher
- Basic internal and external customer service concepts
- Goal setting
- Listening for understanding and accepting constructive criticism
- Conflict resolution to create win/win agreements
- Scientific method of problem solving which serves as the foundation for continuous improvement
- Conduct meetings
- Administer company's policies and procedures
- Coaching/teaching
- Effective interpersonal skills

As these skills are taught, emphasis needs to be placed upon how they are going to be used in your particular work environment. Ideally a staff member or someone familiar with your TWMS and organization will teach the classes.

As with any skill development there are two components: learning and a behavior change. An accountability procedure to measure a department or organization's effectiveness in using specific skills can also be measured through an employee survey. For example, as these skills are introduced into the work environment, an easy measurement system can be implemented to determine the extent the supervisor and department are using the particular skill. The intensity measure may be a simple "yes" or "no"—or offer more choices as the Likert scales we have been discussing in this book. The important point is to measure use! But don't rely on classroom training to create the corporate culture described in the TWMS. The best classroom for learning is the natural work environment, which is the topic of our next section.

Teaching in the Natural Environment

The third suggested procedure to make the TWMS live in the work environment is to teach it in the natural environment. Managers are responsible for teaching both the technical skills needed to produce the service or product and for teaching those behaviors listed in the TWMS.

Now it's time to show you a simple model that you can use to change behavior in the work environment. I would like to have had the intriguing ingenuity for creating the model, but I did not.

My wife is a school psychologist and her professional trade association was sponsoring a speech that I needed to attend to accumulate continuing education hours for my license. My first thought was, "What would a school psychologist discussing the subject of teaching social skills to children offer that would be of interest to me?"

As I lackadaisically listened, it suddenly occurred to me that teaching social skills is exactly what we are doing in organizations. Needless to say, the speaker got my attention once I determined we were interested in the same subject.

I tell you that story for a reason other than to give credit where credit is due. We can learn something from just about anyone if we will do a paradigm shift and "look for what this person can teach me."

Stop and Think Model

Whenever an incident occurs, employees are asked to "Stop and Think" about good and bad choices before responding. Select a choice, implement it and evaluate progress. The model follows:

The Model

Incident: Specify the behavior that occurred.

Stop and Think

Good Choices   **Bad Choices**

    1. _____   1. _____

    2. _____   2. _____

Select a Choice:

Implement:

Evaluate:

To illustrate how the model works and how it is used as a teaching tool, let's use an incident where one employee approaches another employee who is up to his eyeballs in alligators, and demands assistance from this employee immediately. This incident was discussed with employees who brainstormed the alternatives and processed the following agreement to be implemented in the natural work environment.

Incident: One employee demands assistance from another employee.

Stop and Think

Good Choices:

1. Stop and help.
2. Smile, listen and say you'll assist them when you can.
3. Listen and then tell the coworker you can assist them in 30 minutes, so you can finish working with this alligator.

Bad Choices:

1. Tell the employee to get lost.
2. Get mad: "You stupid jerk, can't you see I'm busy?"
3. Talk ugly about the coworker after he leaves.

Selected Choice: The third Good Choice.

Implement: Practice the selected choice.

Feedback: Staff agreed to provide immediate feedback to each other by positively recognizing use of the selected choice and offer a "Stop and Think" reminder when a coworker forgets to implement the agreed upon choice. Progress of using the selected choice can also be evaluated at a subsequent staff meeting.

In this particular incident, the staff added another component as illustrated below.

Incident: Whenever one employee needs another employee who is currently fighting alligators.

Stop and Think

Good Choice:

1. Ask the employee when she can assist with another alligator.

Bad Choice:

1. Demand the employee assist with another alligator.

Selected Choice: The requesting employee has the responsibility to be considerate of the other person's involvement in fighting alligators.

Evaluate: To be scheduled at a subsequent staff meeting.

The objectives in using this model are four-fold:

1. Standardize working procedures to facilitate harmony in the work environment.

2. Provide an easy tool so employees can provide feedback to each other.

3. Encourage employees to exercise self-control, to stop and think before responding.

4. Provide a user friendly procedure for teaching in the natural environment.

During any given day, there are ample opportunities to teach with this model in the natural environment. Employees can use this procedure to define desired behaviors and provide immediate feedback to each other. Or, whenever a supervisor observes another employee selecting "Bad Choices" the observing supervisor can coach the employee about selecting a "Good Choice." Additionally, this tool can also be used by employees to offer a friendly reminder to their supervisor when she is behaving inconsistently with the TeamWork Mission Statement.

Coaching and the TeamWork Mission Statement

The coaching process has rightfully become fashionable for on-the-job training to learn the technical skills associated with an employee's job responsibilities. Coaching involves the following steps:

1. Define the skills to be taught.
2. Explain the importance of learning the skills to be taught.
3. Show how the behavior is to be completed.
4. Observe while the person (student) practices.
5. Provide immediate and specific feedback.

Teaching people (social) skills in the natural environment is a little more difficult for the following reasons:

- Social behaviors to be taught are not well defined.
- People are reluctant to discuss social behaviors out of fear of hurting the employee's feelings or the fear that as a supervisor "I don't know how to discuss such behaviors."

The beauty of the Stop and Think process is that it offers an excellent user-friendly tool to overcome the natural resistance of not wanting to confront an individual regarding his social behaviors.

To illustrate how Coaching, Stop and Think and the TeamWork Mission Statement complement each other, let's use an example from the old management school of thought that continues to plague today's work environment. *"I'm your boss and I will tell you what to do!"*

We previously addressed this behavior with a TWMS value statement—"We are free to express our ideas" and identified the following behaviors to successfully encourage employees to express their ideas:

1. Ask for employee input.
2. Use teams.
3. Listen and accept what is said.

Define the skills to be taught.

In this case, the behaviors listed above are the skills to be taught.

Explain the importance of learning the skills to be taught.

Some obvious reasons to encourage expression of employee's behaviors are:

- New and better ideas
- Increases ownership
- Improves morale
- Increases personal motivation
- Improves team functioning, productivity and quality

Show how it is done.

The up-line supervisor has excellent opportunities to model asking for employee input during department meetings and whenever an employee brings a problem to supervisor.

First, let's address department meetings. Structure staff input by asking employees to discuss pros and cons to reach a consensus during the decision-making process. Another procedure is to ask one or more employees to make recommendations on defined issues. In doing so, these individuals may need to solicit input from their respective staffs. This procedure has the advantage of soliciting input from two levels of staff.

A word of caution is in order: old habits die hard. If your staff meetings have been the ritual boring types of sharing selected information and presenting a laundry list of "already made" decisions, then changing the structure to encourage staff participation may require some patience on your part. You will be tempted to regress to earlier behaviors. Remember this is the cue to—Stop and Think.

Staff meetings become a classroom to model employee involvement and to discuss progress associated with structuring employee input throughout the organization. The manager peer group can be a great educational aid to share ideas.

A second opportunity is employee problems. Here is a great opportunity to solicit input that managers often miss. Most managers teach their employees to bring them problems by readily acting as a paid problem solver. Doing so teaches the employee to think only one thought whenever encountering a problem, "Boss, what do I do now?" The first words spoken by the manager needs to be, "What do you think ought to be done?" In this case, whenever an employee approaches the manager and asks for a problem to be solved, the manager needs to remind the employee to Stop and Think and ask for a recommendation.

Or, whenever an employee sees the manager automatically getting ready to solve the problem, the employee needs to only ask the manager to Stop and Think.

Observe and provide immediate feedback.

Up-line supervisors need to attend down-line supervisor staff meetings and observe how the supervisors deal with their employees in the work environment. Whenever the up-line supervisor observes the down-line supervisor making decisions for employees or otherwise discouraging employee input, the up-line supervisor needs to remind the manager to Stop and Think and discuss the behavior appropriate to that situation which will solicit employee input.

On the other hand, a "You did great soliciting employee input" needs to be shared immediately as well. Actually, the up-line supervisor can also tell the employee, "You did a wonderful job in providing input into the situation." In this scenario, everyone is doing a great job creating the corporate culture of encouraging employee input! Now teaching and learning are occurring in the natural environment where it will do the most good.

This time let's use the chronic problem that plagues most organizations: the failure to listen actively. Everyone will give lip service to its importance, but few people practice listening skillfully because they are too busy talking.

Define the skills to be taught.

The major ingredients of active listening are as follows:

1. Refrain from opening your mouth and listen to what is being said.
2. Rephrase what you heard to ensure understanding.
3. Refrain from interrupting and letting your mind wonder to other subject matter.
4. Let the other person know you are listening via eye contact and appropriate head gestures.
5. Pay attention to body language to learn more about the emotional content of the message.

Explain the importance of learning the skills to be taught.

The reasons to listen actively are:

- To learn the other person's point of view
- You may learn something that you don't know

- Learn about a better idea
- Learn more about the speaker
- Show respect to the other person
- Practice active listening to improve listening skills

Show how it is done.

You have the opportunity to model this behavior every time someone speaks to you. Staff meetings again provide an excellent classroom for learning while discussing input into every decision or discussed. After discussing an item, evaluate the listening process. As a group, ask

- Did we listen for understanding?
- Did everyone have an opportunity to provide input?
- What did we learn from each other that changed our personal opinion on the matter?

Observe and provide immediate feedback.

Up-line supervisors have ample opportunities to observe their staff practicing active listening. Every discussion with a staff member is an opportunity to observe, as well as listening in staff meetings. Plus up-line supervisors can attend down-line supervisor's staff meetings, as well as watch their supervisors listen to their staff on the work floor, break room or outside smoking a cigarette. This is one skill where you don't have to worry about opportunities to observe.

To create an active listening environment ask those who work with you to remind you to Stop and Think whenever they perceive you not actively listening. And you can do the same with them.

Of course, the up-line supervisor needs to quickly say, "You did a great job listening" when observing one of the staff implementing the skill. Additionally, everyone can say, "Thank you for listening to me" whenever they have been the recipient of active listening.

Conducting Annual Evaluations of the TWMS

This is the fourth suggested procedure to make the TWMS live in your work environment. At this point, I only need to remind you of our previous discussion regarding remeasuring both the organization and individual supervisors on the TWMS value statements. Doing so provides excellent feedback by measuring progress. This procedure also establishes these behaviors as integral characteristics of the corporate culture.

In Summary

We discussed four processes to feed the growth of your TWMS.

1. Regularly scheduling customer service meetings.
2. Walking the talk of the TWMS, then leading by example.
3. Teaching in the natural environment.
4. Evaluating the organization and supervisors annually in terms of the TWMS.

Implementing these processes will undoubtedly create a learning environment for your organization. In doing so, your organization will have the necessary self-discipline, focus and energy to implement quality improvement processes including reengineering and improvement to customer service levels. Your employees realize, without question, their importance to your company's success. Consequently, the commitment will be there to drive the company's success to higher levels.

Living the change is the only way

for the change to become permanent.

❖9❖

A Candid Conversation with the CEO

What You Will Learn

This chapter offers suggestions to help you lead the change effort.

The End Near or Just the Beginning?

You have completed reading about a structured, comprehensive, data-based decision-making process. Now it is time to quit reading about it, and *do* what it takes to create the corporate culture you want for your organization.

You know the benefits of creating a better, more dynamic organization. You know the price you might pay for avoiding the frustration associated with change. Remember the frog? You know that it is up to you to begin at the top. Where else can true change begin?

The question is: are you willing to begin change with *you*?

I certainly do not mean to dampen your enthusiasm for the process, but most of the people in your organization probably believe that any major change effort will end up just like the last ones did—dead!

From a selfish standpoint, I have no interest in contributing to your idea of the month cemetery. So before you launch a process to change your corporate culture, please do some serious soul searching.

Are You Ready to Change?

Question	Answer Yes	No
1. Am I willing to change more than other managers and employees?	☐	☐
2. Am I willing to subject myself to suggested improvements and be rated by those I supervise?	☐	☐
3. Am I willing to stay focused on the change process?	☐	☐
4. Will I hold my staff accountable to what we decide to implement?	☐	☐
5. Will my staff do whatever is necessary to implement real and lasting change?	☐	☐

If your answer is "No" to any of the above questions, then you need to consider whether you are serious enough about the change process to change yourself.

Remember, organizations don't change until people do. And that change always starts at the top. Many CEOs believe that change is always for someone else. The leader in the organization (and each department for that matter) must lead the change process or it will not occur.

I'm asking you to be the leader of change.

Assuming you want to proceed, then let me offer a few more suggestions for the management structure that will help all of you to live your TeamWork Mission

Statement. I suppose the following list could be called "Manager's Reminders," as it offers a summary of many of the things we discussed.

Manager's Reminders

- Discuss the implementation of your TWMS action steps with your staff.
- Discuss the implementation of your staff's TWMS action steps with their staff.
- Evaluate progress of your TWMS action steps with your staff.
- Evaluate progress your staff has achieved to successfully implement the TWMS action steps with their staff and decide what you can do to assist them.
- Attend department meetings throughout the organization to discuss the change effort.
- Communicate all progress throughout the organization.
- Walk the talk of the TWMS and ask your staff to let you know when you do not use the Stop and Think coaching model.
- Test your staff by purposefully acting in contradiction to your TWMS to ensure they will give you feedback when you do not walk the talk of the TWMS.
- Visit with employees and inquire what they have done to improve internal customer service today.
- Ask employees to tell you what the TWMS means to them.
- Talk to employees in the hallways and break rooms about the change effort and solicit feedback on progress.

- Recognize those who have made progress with a sincere pat on the back.

In Summary

There is little doubt that your organization will change as time goes by. The decision you have to make is: are you going to lead the change process? Successful organizational change evolves from individuals who lead the change process by first changing themselves.

Are you ready?

Can you lead by example?

If the answer is yes to both questions, then get out there and get with it. And *good luck.*

Setting a good example is one

of the more difficult assignments in life.

❖ *Index* ❖

T

V

W

Give the Gift of Leadership Excellence to Your Friends and Colleagues

CHECK YOUR LEADING BOOKSTORE
OR ORDER BELOW

☐ **YES**, I want _____ copies of *Frustration Is Your Organization's Best Friend* at $12.95 each, plus $3 shipping per book (Arkansas residents please add 78¢ state sales tax per book). Canadian orders must be accompanied by a postal money order in U.S. funds. Allow 15 days for delivery.

☐ **YES**, I am interested in having **Larry Cole** speak or give a seminar to my company, association, school, or organization. Please send information.

My check or money order for $_____ is enclosed.
Please charge my ☐ Visa ☐ MasterCard

Name _____ Phone _____

Organization _____

Address _____

City/State/Zip _____

Card # _____ Exp. Date _____

Signature _____

Please make your check payable and return to:
LifeSkills Publishers
5 Towering Pines
Conway, AR 72032

Or call your credit card order to: (800) 709-6778
or fax your order to: (501) 327-4116